PRAISE FOR

INTROVERT REVOLUTION

Introvert Revolution is a clarion call to open the eyes and ears of introverts and extroverts alike. In this bias-busting book, Andy Johnson contends, "one of the biggest challenges lies in reframing perceived weaknesses as strengths and allowing ourselves to reject culturally imposed standards of leadership." Introverts contribute something important to the world as leaders, as history attests. Johnson shares how they can do so authentically, powerfully—and even quietly—amid our noisy world.

— **Nancy Ancowitz, Author of** *Self-Promotion for Introverts®*

As an ambivert, I am constantly learning to how to recognize and optimize the balance of my introverted and extroverted traits. Andy Johnson's book provided me with deep and actionable insights to become a more complete leader and coach. I strongly encourage you to join this life changing revolution!

— **Scott Howard, Manager Big Data Delivery, Hewlett-Packard**

This well researched and compelling read makes the case for introverted leadership in a unique way. Author Andy Johnson draws upon his own early career struggles blended with case studies and hard science to help introverts draw upon their authentic "yin" selves. He lays out a map for introverts to take courageous and practical steps to ramp up their leadership game.

— **Jennifer Kahnweiler, Ph. D., Author of** *The Introverted Leader: Building on Your Quiet Strength, Quiet Influence: The Introvert's Guide to Making a Difference* **and** *The Genius of Opposites: How Introverts and Extroverts Achieve Extraordinary Results Together*

Through a rich mix of storytelling, cultural analysis and scientific studies, *Introvert Revolution* helps introverted leaders reclaim and stand on the firm ground of who they are -- strengths, vulnerabilities and all, bringing wisdom and needed balance to our lopsided yang culture.

— Laurie Helgoe, Ph.D., Psychologist and Author of *Introvert Power: Why Your Inner Life is Your Hidden Strength*

For decades the prevailing models of leadership have placed a premium on what would be identified as extroverted behavior--charisma, likeability, media appeal, promotional skills, and salesmanship. In *Introvert Revolution* Andy Johnson validates the leadership potential and contribution of introverts and recommends a model that balances the extroverted *yang* with the introverted *yin*. He helps us understand how to tap what is perhaps the most underutilized talent pool in our organizations--the introverts. With Johnson's help, introverts can stop "faking it until they make it" and find ways to make a difference without having to be different.

— Gordon Holland, Talent Manager, Western States Equipment Company

Too many introverted leaders feel constrained to lead and live inauthentically. Trying to be someone other than yourself is detrimental to health and well-being as well as leadership effectiveness. In *Introvert Revolution*, author Andy Johnson explains the pressure created in the West for introverted leaders to pretend to be extroverts and to downplay their natural strengths and temperament. Living under the weight of this cultural bias has a detrimental effect on these leaders as well as the organizations they serve. Andy provides a deep analysis of this bias and of its effects. What I like is that he reinforces both the personal accountability as well as a path for these introverted leaders to move toward greater authenticity. I highly recommend this book for introverted leaders and those who work with them to create workplaces where all of us work with greater inspiration and engagement.

— Henna Inam, CEO of Transformational Leadership Inc. and Author of *Wired for Authenticity: Seven Practices to Inspire, Adapt and Lead*

Leading **authentically** in a world that says you can't.

INTROVERT

ANDY JOHNSON

For further information about speaking engagements, professional consultation, special bulk pricing, or other related inquiries, see www.introvertrevolution.com.

Print ISBN: 978-1-61206-100-9
eBook ISBN: 978-1-61206-106-1

Interior design by: Fusion Creative Works, fusioncw.com
Cover design by: Studio A, artbystudioA.com

Published by

AlohaPublishing.com
First Printing
Printed in the United States of America

This book is dedicated to all the *yin* leaders who have gone before, influencing through quiet strength. In their own way, they have shown us a path of true leadership centered on character that transcends the current cultural milieu and noise. In particular, to my brother-in-law, Phil, who has quietly and faithfully led my sister and his family by serving them for over thirty-one years. You are an example of the strengths I describe in this book. You exemplify the attributes of a successful, yin leader who combines strength and genuine humility.

CONTENTS

PART THREE: RETAKING THE STAGE

APPENDICES

FIGURES

TABLES

"Groups famously follow the opinions of the most dominant or charismatic person in the room, even though there's zero correlation between being the best talker and having the best ideas—I mean zero."

— **Susan Cain, author of *Quiet: The Power of Introverts in a World That Can't Stop Talking*, from her 2012 TED Talk**

A NOTE ON BIAS

We all have biases. It is part and parcel of the human condition. Once we acknowledge our biases, the next healthy thing to do is to minimize their impact on others. I have sought to do that in the pages that follow (with the help of both extroverted and introverted female editors). I recognize, however, that eliminating bias entirely is not possible and that some of mine have leaked through onto these pages.

I have many biases of which I am aware, some of which are relevant to mention:

- **Male**—Most of the significant people in my life have been female. I think I understand femaleness better than most males. Having said this, I'm sure I still have blind spots related to my gender that female readers might notice. In some ways, however, I may actually be female-biased due to my background.

- **White**—Though I identify with the struggle of different groups that have suffered at the hands of white oppressors, I am sure I still have some degree of white bias. I am attempting to continue to move toward greater self-awareness as it relates to my ethnicity and the advantages I have had simply as a result of the color of my skin.

- **Introverted**—This book is based on the premise that Western culture is significantly biased in favor of extroversion. I have experienced many painful things in life at the expense of extroverts, well-meaning or not, and have suffered because of this cultural bias. While I am likely also biased because of my introversion, my belief remains that extroversion is not the problem and that introversion, ambiversion, and extroversion are all differing temperaments of psychologically healthy people and great leaders.

In light of these biases, I offer my willingness to be called out on any unfair statements I have made in this book and to be accountable to you, the reader, for any negative impact my biases have on you.

INTRODUCTION

August 11, 1965

Los Angeles in the 1950s and '60s was a city waiting to explode. William H. Parker, the chief of police, was famous for using fear and intimidation, ruling the city with power and an iron fist. The thin blue line was known for harassing young black teenagers and letting them know who was boss. Tension between law enforcement and the black community was ever increasing and always present.

In 1963, the California legislature passed the Rumford Fair Housing Act. The act was intended to end racial discrimination by property owners and landlords who refused to rent or sell to "colored" people. Prior to its passage, restrictive covenants preventing African American and Hispanic people from buying and renting property in certain areas were common. But despite good intentions, the act only served to increase the racial tension in south LA. In response, conservative political groups gathered together to sponsor Proposition 14 a year later, which would, in effect, nullify the Rumford Act. The initiative passed with a sixty-five percent approval. California had voted to reject the concept of fair housing.

Soon after the passage of Prop 14, the federal government cut off all housing funds to California. The tension between the black and white communities was at an all-time high. The city was full of fuel, just waiting for a spark to fall.

IGNITING WATTS

The summer of 1965 had been unusually hot. On August 11, Marquette Frye, a twenty-one-year-old African American man, was driving his mother's 1955 Buick, his only means of transportation. His brother, Ronald, was in the car with him. Unfortunately, Frye, the driver, had consumed a few beers earlier that afternoon.

Just outside of Watts, Marquette was pulled over by the California Highway Patrol for suspicion of driving while intoxicated. While his partner interviewed Marquette and conducted a field sobriety test, Lee Minikus, a white CHP officer, radioed for the Buick to be impounded. Ronald Frye, Marquette's brother, meanwhile walked two blocks to the family's home to fetch the boys' mother, Rena Price.

By the time Rena arrived on the scene, so had a crowd of more than two hundred bystanders. Upon her arrival, Rena scolded her son for driving drunk. Marquette started resisting arrest, and he and the officers began to scuffle on the corner of Avalon Blvd. and 116th Street. The situation rapidly escalated.[1]

Accounts of what happened next vary, but here's one account. Someone shoved Rena. Marquette was struck by one of the officers. Rena responded in her son's defense, jumping on one of the officers. One of the officers pulled out a shotgun. People in the community were watching intently. Rumors spread like wildfire, some founded, some not: "The police roughed up Price. They kicked a pregnant woman." Frye, his brother and mother were all arrested and taken into custody. A feeling of unrest settled in among the community. In reality, a spark had been ignited and lay still smoldering, ready to ignite the frustrated residents of Watts.

No one knows where exactly it began. Later that evening, LAPD officers were attacked with rocks and chunks of concrete. Buildings were set on fire. Forty-six square miles of south Los Angeles became a combat zone in a battle that would continue for six days. The California Army National Guard was called in to restore peace in the midst of this uprising against an oppressive system.[2]

That same day the riots began, August 11, 26 miles to the east of Watts, at the small and inconsequential Intercommunity Hospital in Covina, California, a son, the youngest of four children, was born to a white middle class couple. The husband, age 31, was an architect. The wife and fourth-time mother, age 29, was a homemaker. This child was a blessed "accident." Nonetheless, the young couple was glad to welcome their new son into their family. As labor began, they somewhat routinely made their fourth trek to the hospital. Labor progressed, as it had before, throughout the course of a long day.

It was now late afternoon and the baby was finally here. As he emerged, the delivery room was filled with a flurry of activity, the kind that comes from a newborn in distress. The baby was blue. His lung had collapsed and he was not getting adequate oxygen. The delivering physician, following his training protocol, attempted to inflate the lung by gently blowing air through a tube inserted into the infant. It didn't work. Instead of the lung inflating, now there was a tear in it. The newborn in an ambulance and his anxious father following in another vehicle left the Covina hospital heading west down the 10 freeway. As they approached downtown Los Angeles, they were diverted off of the 10 for fear of sniper fire. They both eventually arrived at Children's Hospital, a location eleven miles north of the epicenter of the Watts riots that had erupted earlier that evening.

Born in the midst of chaos and upheaval in Los Angeles, this last child in a middle-class white family seemed to have an invisible connection to the unrest in Watts. That child, powerless at birth and unable to breathe on his own, would have a different form of powerlessness as he grew. Some forms of being "one down" are easier to see than others. For the people of Watts, societal mistreatment was external, visible and overt. For the baby, it would be harder to recognize. While the baby and mother recovered in the hospital, the city did not. By the time the violence subsided, the community had suffered forty million dollars in property damage. There were 3,438 arrests and thirty-four deaths. An estimated thirty-five thousand adults had participated in the riots. The six-day unrest was national news.

A sense of powerlessness laid under the growing frustration in Watts. On August 17, six days after the riots began, Dr. Martin Luther King Jr. arrived in California. King cited environmental rather than racial causes for the riot. He focused his comments on the problems of economic deprivation, social isolation, inadequate housing, and general despair in the black community. King famously said that the riots in Watts were "the beginning of a stirring of a deprived people in a society who have been bypassed by the progress of the past decade."[3]

Being looked down on and bypassed in regard to opportunity deeply impacted the black community in south LA. They were on the losing end of the racial stereotypes dominating the culture of Southern California. Stereotypes allow those in power to rationalize and justify ongoing mistreatment and marginalization.

LEADERSHIP STEREOTYPES

Stereotypes are nasty, stubborn, frustrating and hurtful things. They leave those on the receiving end often feeling misunderstood, marginalized and devalued. I vividly recall feeling that way due to my introverted nature.

I work as an executive coach who specializes in working with introverted leaders. As an introvert myself, I understand the cultural challenges my clients tend to face. The dominant stereotype in the West that connects leadership and extroversion eliminates more than half of the population, leaving just an extroverted few who have the requisite personality traits thought to be necessary for leading others. I recall one such experience that left me feeling the effects of this bias.

A few years ago, I attended a conference related to my executive coaching work. I sat down at the banquet one evening, a highlight of the three-day conference, after a long day of meetings and seminars— things that drain energy from an introvert like myself. I was mentally fatigued and really looking forward to a good meal, a glass of wine, and some relaxed interaction with a close friend. These are the things that recharge my batteries and renew me. As is typical, the banquet had us sitting at tables of ten, which meant meeting and interacting with new people, eight of them, something that takes work for an introvert. Getting past the initial awkwardness that can exist between people who don't know each other, an extrovert at our table broke the ice.

He went on to explain that he was a consultant, detailing his particular niche and focus. Each person, in turn, did similarly. The conversation was naturally progressing in a circle. I had done the math. My turn was next.

"I'm an executive coach focused on working with what I call *quiet leaders*, introverts and ambiverts. I focus on the unique strengths and challenges of these more introverted leaders," I said. The silence was palpable, followed by grins and snickers. A table of people in the leadership development business found it humorous to connect the words *introvert* and *leader*. The conversation continued as others introduced themselves, yet I felt the sting of the previous interaction. It played over in my head. I could still see their faces and feel the rejection caused by their questioning the legitimacy of my assumption, that introverts and ambiverts could in fact *be* leaders. I felt an all-too familiar feeling of being out of place at the table.

Since that evening, I've thought deeply, something introverts are prone to do, about my reaction and what it said about the stereotype of leadership that existed at that table.

What is leadership? What are the qualities or skills a good leader has as opposed to a bad leader or a non-leader? These are questions I take up with groups of introverted leaders in a two-day intensive training called *Yin* Leader Workshop. The list of qualities that is developed is remarkably consistent with each group that does the exercise. Qualities like *character, humility, discipline, integrity, selflessness, clarity, goal-oriented, higher-cause driven, moral courage, authenticity (not phony), self-awareness, empathy,* and *good communication* all seem to end up on the flip chart.

What's missing from this list? Notably absent are traits like *charismatic, outgoing, promoter, salesman, driven, aggressive, powerful,* and *fast paced*—all extroverted traits.

I then typically ask the workshop group if they see a disconnect between the list of leadership qualities and the cultural myth of type A or charismatic leaders. It is an aha moment for most in the group. "You mean there's not something wrong with me, something that disqualifies me from being a leader?" one says. "I don't see anything on that list that I can't be," another adds.

The conversation over dinner that night left a bad taste in my mouth, pun intended. It reflected the existence of what Susan Cain has called the *extrovert ideal*.[4] The extrovert ideal, the myth of the charismatic leader, the hero or the great man is a cultural stereotype in the West, and particularly the United States, about what a leader looks like. [5] Unfortunately, this pervasive bias leaves introverts and ambiverts (those displaying both introverted and extroverted qualities), with our quiet consent if we're not careful, out of the leadership picture.[6]

The struggle for racial equality has been extremely difficult and continues to this day. People have been horribly mistreated and marginalized simply for the color of their skin. The terror they have faced has often come in the form of unthinkable acts of violence and other atrocities. To a lesser degree and with a different approach, introverted leaders are also frequently left watching the advances of others, being bypassed and not benefitting from the progress in our organizations or society at large. The struggle for leadership equality, perhaps more similar to the women's movement than to Watts, is a fight marked by more subtle forms of oppression. When introverts are held back by cultural biases, both the introverts themselves and the organizations they serve suffer losses—of opportunity and the failure to benefit from the full exercise of our unique strengths, respectively.

INTROVERT REVOLUTION

What can we do? How can we respond to biases and imbalances that leave whole groups of people behind? How can we counter those persistent stereotypes that make us feel so misunderstood? Reform, changing the *status quo*, is possible, though difficult, when the system is open to degrees of change. Revolution, however, becomes necessary when the system is closed, when those in power become oppressive enough and sufficiently resistant to change that those under their domination see no alternative but to revolt.

The root problems in Watts were powerlessness and marginalization. The dominant class, white, had conspired to keep the black community "one down," trapped in a less than socio-economic class. The power of the white majority was embodied and embedded in the social and cultural structures of Southern California, including the LAPD. Truth or doing the right thing no longer controlled; it was the biased white perspective, filled with all kinds of inaccurate stereotypes, that was determinative. As a result, the black population in Watts missed out on the progress of the society all around them. They were passed by and left with a less-than-good taste in their mouths, similar to but far stronger than the bad taste I had in my mouth at a table of extroverts who didn't seem to get me.

We are all born into an existing cultural context. While we can choose some aspects of our lives, many of the variables are dealt to us at the outset. Red, yellow, black, white, male, female, we don't get to choose. So it is with this trait called introversion (or ambiversion), at least fifty percent of which is hereditary and genetic.[7] All of us who are born this way, who don't fit the Western ideal of extroversion, are on the wrong side of the power equation. That is how it has been in American culture since at least the beginning of the twentieth century.

Cultural revolution is always hard work. There are things we can do, for those who have ears to hear and eyes to see, to advance the cause of diversity and equality in our society. Systems, however, are set up to maintain and reinforce the status quo. Established systems of power and privilege understandably resist change; the beneficiaries don't want to lose their advantages.

While society at large may or may not make progress in recognizing the strengths of introversion, we, as introverted leaders, at the very least have an opportunity to change ourselves. This is no small task, however. The path toward empowered authentic leadership as introverts is a reversal of the long, winding road we followed to get here. For as many years as we have been on the planet and immersed in this culture, we have been receiving messages. We've taken them in through our eyes and ears, stored them in our brains and hearts, and thought deeply and consistently about them. These messages have been about who we are and what we are capable of, our identity.

Who are you? What makes you the unique, gifted and capable person you are? What are you adding to your circles of relationships? What strengths do you bring to the table? Why is your leadership needed in your organization?

Perhaps the prominent model for understanding an introvert's *cultural identity* is the model advanced by Atkinson, Morten and Sue.[8] Cultural identity? Introversion? You may not think of it in those terms now, but soon you will. Introversion and extroversion are, in many ways, two different cultures, even two different worlds. Introverts make progress toward self-acceptance by passing through recognizable stages along the way toward fully embracing their cultural identity.

THE STAGES OF INTROVERTED IDENTITY

Embracing who we are and were made to be happens in stages. We all tend to begin with a similar naiveté and a lack of understanding about this aspect of self. The light usually dawns slowly and in the midst of external influences helping us to move forward. Often this movement toward identity is accompanied with the pain that brings change.

Stage one is called *conformity*. Initially, you identify with the dominant culture (the extrovert ideal). You learn, internalize and assume the cultural stereotype concerning extroversion and have no real desire or thought about an alternative (introversion). Characteristics of this stage include numbness, non-feeling and lack of awareness. Your introversion is not something you are aware of and not perceived as a problem yet. You don't yet identify with it. It's not you.

Stage two is *dissonance*. At some point, you encounter a catalyst that makes you question the extroverted cultural bias.. Perhaps you are passed over for yet another promotion. Or you have a difficult interaction with a new over-the-top extroverted supervisor. Or you may just have completed an assessment and are surprised to hear the word introvert applied to you. Characteristics of this stage include anger, fear, sadness, surprise and reactivity. You are becoming aware that you are introverted and that some people around you don't appreciate it. This causes conflict in your head between who you are and how you are supposed to be or act.

Stage three is *resistance*. As a result of this catalyst, you begin to withdraw somewhat from the extrovert-biased culture around you and explore your identity as introverted. Characteristics of this stage include anger, sadness, grief and contemplativeness. You may be perceived by those around you as unnecessarily or inappropriately angry about "nothing." They may tell you to "get over it." You, at this point, might become somewhat hard to live or work with.

Stage four is *introspection*. You think and reflect deeply on this growing self-identity and begin to reintegrate your newfound self into the dominant culture without compromising your authentic you. Characteristics of this stage include beginnings of feeling empowered, hopefulness and thoughtfulness. You will likely be less volatile and less easily triggered as you talk about the cultural problem or yourself. Your message will begin to transmit more effectively with those around you.

Stage five includes synergistic *articulation* and *awareness*. You eventually experience your optimal identity. You are now able to identify and appreciate both cultures (extroverted and introverted) and balance all aspects of your true self and your introverted nature in the world around you. Characteristics of this stage include awareness, calmness, respectfulness, feeling invigorated and empowered, authenticity, and congruence. You are becoming whole.

I have always been and remain an introvert. I lived, however, for forty-three years in the conformity stage (stage one) of cultural identity development, not acknowledging this important personal trait in myself. My father was a strong extrovert as was my oldest brother. The family values seemed to favor extroversion. I had absorbed that stereotype as well. It wasn't until I took some assessments and read a few timely books that I began to experience some dissonance.

There was always a nagging dull sense that something wasn't quite right from childhood. I was a great student (a "brain" as I was unaffectionately called in high school), felt things deeply and valued honesty and doing what was right to a fault. I didn't understand the contrary feelings that somehow I was deficient, that something was wrong with me, that somehow I didn't quite measure up. In fact, for many of those first forty-three years, I thought I was an extrovert, acted like one as often as I could and came up as one on tests measuring for the trait. I've been on an identity journey ever since I began to discover that what I was experiencing had a name. It's called introversion. This is the journey I invite you to join me on.

This five-stage journey toward awareness and authenticity is informed by new ways of thinking, feeling and being. Reversing those beliefs, retracing our steps, and taking a different direction is not easy work. There is no quick fix for an identity developed over the course of a lifetime. To work back out of our current paradigm, we'll follow the opposite route on our journey together. *Introvert Revolution* lays out a path for you to follow.

In *part one*, you'll begin by understanding the stage of life on which we perform, the contrast between two very different worlds. East (*yin*) and West (*yang*) represent two contrasting ways of seeing the human condition and society in general. Both bring insight and differing perspectives to the conversation. You'll begin to see that part of the problem introverts face is cultural and contextual; you've been living in a world that validates the other side of the equation. Optimally, a societal balance between these two complementary halves can be found, affirmed and embraced. You'll end part one by thinking about the nature of a good life.

Once you understand the stage you're on, you'll then begin to rethink your part in the play in *part two*. You'll begin by bringing truth to counter current cultural myths. Separating fiction from fact about the real nature of introversion is the first step toward wholeness. Truth is one of the greatest weapons you have in this bloodless revolution. From there, you'll reexamine the nature-nurture debate as it relates to introversion. You need to understand not only your physiological differences but also the cumulative effect of many years and various levels of related rejection to be able to turn the tide in favor of acceptance. Your journey explores the depths of social pain and the likelihood of gaining an unwelcome friend on the journey, shame.

In *part three*, you'll apply your new insights into culture, yourself and past experiences and directly re-approach the subject of leadership. This is your call to action. While you may have been playing a mismatched part for some time, you'll now take up a new role that has been typecast to fit you perfectly. You'll ask and answer important questions: Why do we need leadership balance in our organizations? What does introverted leadership look like? What strengths do quiet leaders bring to the table? And lastly and most importantly, how can we embrace who we are (as opposed to trying to be someone else) and lead confidently and authentically to make our world a better place? Learning to lead *as yourself* is the ultimate goal.

Do you remember the child born in the midst of the Watts riots? He was powerless to breathe on his own at birth and would grow up to face many additional challenges throughout life. *Being himself, however, would prove to be his greatest challenge.*

That child with the hole in his lung, taken to Children's Hospital the night of the Watts riots, is me. My lung healed itself that day, and I've been alive and somewhat well ever since. What connects me, a six-foot two-inch, white, highly educated, and otherwise privileged male, to the situation in Watts? Not much. I have almost every advantage in Western society, except one. I'm an introvert.

While I certainly cannot and would not equate the struggles I have experienced at birth or throughout life with the struggles of living as an African American in 1960s south Los Angeles, for different reasons and with different intensities, we have both experienced the sting of being marginalized. There is common ground between all groups that, for whatever reason, have been mistreated, oppressed or held back. Minorities, women, the poor, certain religious groups, introverts, and other marginalized groups have something in common. We share an invisible, regrettable yet empathic connection.

Introvert Revolution takes you on a journey toward becoming the authentic leader our teams or organizations need. This book is about a *personal revolution*, an internal transformation of the way you view yourself as a person and as a leader. This is a struggle against the current. You are swimming upstream and so you must work diligently until our society begins to shift back toward balance. While you await the cultural transformation you hope and work for, you discover that what you can control is yourself. You can revolt against the culture and its impact on you personally and become the leader, in the fullest sense, you were destined to be. As an introvert, a professional counselor and an executive coach, it is my privilege to lead other introverts on this journey. We begin our journey appropriately with a discussion of culture, the stream we find ourselves in. Safe travels.

Andy Johnson
Nampa, Idaho 2015

The Stage of Life

"All the world's a stage . . ."

—William Shakespeare

Imagine yourself as part of the world's greatest heavy metal band.[1]
You're the lead singer and play electric guitar. On top of that you've got
a killer voice and have everything that goes along with the look a heavy
metal artist should have. You've got the right hair, clothes, tattoos and
attitude. You're not alone. Every member of your band is the real thing,
hard core. You're in London to perform for an audience of thousands at
Wembley Stadium. You've warmed up, the crew has gotten the smoke ma-
chines going and lights flashing, and the curtain begins to part.

As the curtain opens, you begin to see things that surprise you. You
didn't expect to see nearly as many men in suits and ties. And the few
women who are there look different than your typical audience, a bit up-
tight for your style. As the smoke clears, you become increasingly aware that
something is amiss. This doesn't look anything like a heavy metal crowd.
The announcer for the event comes forward, fanning the remaining smoke

from his face, takes the microphone from your stand and proudly says, "Welcome to this year's Annual Conference of CPAs."

Context matters. For the right crowd, you are who you think you are, the bomb. For the wrong crowd, you stick out like a sore thumb. If your work environment is like a stage, how comfortable are you being you? As an introvert, please understand that in Asia or Scandinavia, you're a rock star. Everything you naturally are is what the culture is seeking. You don't have to become, and wouldn't want to be, anyone other than yourself.

As we'll explore in this section, the yang *culture in which we live doesn't view introverts that way. From the time you took the stage, perhaps you have been trying to lead as someone other than yourself because the culture told you that was required. You may have felt as though you were on the wrong stage, just like a heavy metal band at a CPA conference.*

If the world is a stage, it is culture that defines the nature of the stage on which we perform. We begin in part one by considering the bigger picture, the cultural context in which we experience life as introverted leaders. Do you ever feel like you don't fit? Misunderstood? Do you ever wonder if you were born in the wrong century? Country? Ever feel like a fish out of water? Like the curtain is opening to the wrong audience? These are all aspects of living in a world that is disconnected and ill-fitting in significant ways from who you are. The world is divided into two primary cultures: yin *and* yang. *Understanding these cultural differences is the first step on our journey toward authentic leadership.*

1

Culture

"I don't think culture is something you can describe."

—Bill Gates

Meet Kevin, the betta fish.[1] He's the only pet my daughter is able to keep in her second-story apartment. She is convinced that she has trained him to come in response to the sound of her voice calling his name. Kevin has no idea that he's a fish or that he lives in the confines of a small circular tank in an upstairs window. His world is terribly small, about five gallons of water surrounded by clear plastic with a few brightly colored plastic plants. He doesn't know any different. He's unaware of the water that circulates in his gills, providing the oxygen that he needs to live and flourish.

We're a lot like Kevin. Culture is the water we swim in, the air we breathe. It's hard to define in the same way that the air around us is hard to see. We tend to take it for granted, unless we get a tear in our lung and can't breathe. This thing, air, on which we are completely dependent moment by moment, the invisible substance that brings oxygen into our lungs, is something we enjoy without thinking consciously about. We breathe in. We breathe out. And we do it all, about twenty thousand times a day automatically, passively, reflexively. This is the difficulty in defining and discussing culture. It tends to fly under the radar. Like water circulating in the gills of a fish or air in our lungs, we are unaware of its constancy in our lives.

WHAT IS CULTURE?

For cultural psychologists who study this phenomenon every day, definitions help to bring clarity. Two such psychologists have dedicated their lives and careers to the study of this invisible reality. Hazel Markus and Alana Conner define culture as, "the ideas, institutions and interactions that tell a group of people how to think, feel and act."[2]

Culture is embodied in our shared thoughts, woven into the fabric of our institutions and invisibly shaping all of our discourse. Culture constantly communicates its values and ideals to us through various channels. One of the strongest means of cultural conditioning is the media, a constant source of bias-filled information. It tells us what the "good life" is and how to think about it.

Culture is about *us*, the things we share collectively as a society, a group of people inextricably connected to one another. Culture shapes us in all facets of our lives. This invisible force is larger than any one of us and unavoidably exerts its influence over all of us. And yet, this all occurs primarily without our deliberate attention or permission. We can try to ignore it, but its reality is reinforced in our reaction. In a real sense, culture just happens. We're in a small fish tank in a window overlooking the universe. Culture is flowing through our gills as we swim in it and we're about as aware as Kevin, the betta fish.

Culture is always about *meaning* and *beliefs*. Human beings have an intrinsic need to create meaning and to seek after truth, a coherent sense of the world around us. The largest part of what we believe is located in the realm of assumptions. These core beliefs, though always operative, are usually happening below our level of conscious thought or deliberation. The things we believe most firmly are those unquestioned and unquestionable things that we just know that we know that we know. How do we know these things? In large part, the culture tells us so. Our assumptive world consists of "the assumptions or beliefs that ground, secure or orient people, that give a sense of reality, meaning or purpose to life."[3]

We hold these beliefs and assumptions about the world, ourselves and others. The beliefs we hold about others are often in the form of stereotypes. In order to make decisions more quickly or automatically, we all use certain mental shortcuts. We draw hasty and pre-rational (or irrational) conclusions about someone on the basis of a stereotype, a mental picture that we hold, about "people like that." We say things like "All introverts are shy" or "Introverts don't really like people." Stereotypes are always personal beliefs about *others*. Most of these beliefs go largely unchallenged in the cultural dialogue until someone comes along with new information to challenge the status quo.

Culture is also about *value*.[4] Cultures tend to place a higher priority on some things at the expense of others. Each person has his or her own system of valuing. The person, however, is within a culture that has a tendency to impose its group values on each member. Our society, for example, values extroversion and tends to devalue introversion. We see extroversion as a good and introversion as an ill. This explains why so many introverts are hesitant to self-identify as such.

Interestingly, it is not uncommon for a society to have some dissonance between what they say they believe and what they actually value. Some have identified this gap as a discrepancy between *professed values* and *actual values*.[5] Our true values are most clearly displayed in the things we support with our time, talent or resources. You may, for instance, say you value marriage as an important foundational social institution, but in your actions you may be forced to see you actually value each person's individual happiness more, according to a *yang* influenced worldview.

What we believe and value as a culture, we *practice*. These outward actions make our commonly held assumptions seen. For example, in U.S. culture, we don't just prefer extroversion; we actually promote people within organizations as a reflection of this deeply held belief that extroverts make better leaders. The stories we'll read about in this book are the result of real actions, flowing from deeply and even subconsciously held beliefs reinforced by the culture, taken toward introverted leaders. We put our actions and values into practice.

It doesn't stop there. We don't just have certain cultural practices; we also have a complex system of maintaining conformity to group practices. Culture is also about norms and mores, our *standards*. A norm or a standard is an expectation of acceptable beliefs, values or practices in a group. Everyone needs to somehow be kept on the same page, to do life in a similar way. Some of these norms are embodied in the written law. Others are just as real and operative though unwritten.

So, we not only treat introverts in the workplace according to our values and beliefs, we have invisible group dynamics that assure we will continue to do so. We know we have broken a cultural standard on the basis of our own internal barometer and according to the reactions of others around us. An introvert gets promoted to a leadership position and people in the office murmur about the lack of extroverted traits in the new leader. "She's not positive enough. He's not that outgoing. She doesn't seem driven enough to get the results we need."

Group enforcement of cultural standards comes in different ways and at different levels, and that enforcement is what gives our beliefs and values teeth. One of the most commonly used is the practice of rejection from the in-group. The new introverted leader experiences strange treatment from others on the executive team and puzzles over why he or she seems to be treated so differently. Whether intentional or driven by subconscious beliefs and stereotypes outside of awareness, this is often a means of punishing or shaming the violator of the group standards in an attempt to control his or her future behavior in the group, a way of maintaining the pecking order.

Culture and *language* always go together. Human beings, as differentiated from the animals around them, are communicative creatures by way of language. In fact, researchers have demonstrated that human communication is qualitatively different from any other animals on the planet.[6] Communication, for humans, is the essence of relationship. This explains why groups of people with different languages commonly have differing ideas about how others should think, feel, or act. The words we use and the way we use them are utterly interconnected to this concept of culture.

The way we speak, the language we use, about introversion and extroversion is a constantly shaping force in our society. A news reporter on TV just this morning described a soldier who had become withdrawn from his platoon with the use of the phrase, "He had become more introverted." As we better understand the nature of introversion, it becomes clear that the soldier didn't in fact become more introverted, but likely withdrew (an action) and was possibly feeling depressed or discouraged (feelings). Introversion is not an action or a feeling per se, but rather a temperamental trait, a way of being that remains fairly stable and constant over time. When we use "introverted" as a synonym for "shy" or "withdrawn" or "antisocial," we reinforce the cultural stereotypes with the language we use.

Language often shows up embodied in *story*. Picture yourself in primitive society. Your tribe gathers at night in the cave to share in a pre-television form of entertainment, a story. By the light of the fire, the elder in your tribe tells legends that have been handed down for generations. These tales explain for the tribe how they got there, why they exist and what they are in the world to do. They give meaning, purpose and direction to life. And they are incredibly engaging.

All cultures have stories. From the earliest human history, we have used the power of story to give meaning to life. We have stories about our place in the big picture, often including rich and possibly embellished histories about our past achievements as a group. For each of us, these stories are part of a bigger story that connects us. In many ways, cultural narratives are adaptive, healthy, and critical to our ability to interpret our existence and confirm the truth of our beliefs and values. Our culture in the West, unfortunately, has a story about leadership that suggests the part must be played by an over-the-top extrovert.

We've now come full circle. The cultural stories reinforce the beliefs and values of the culture. In fact, all six of these cultural forces—beliefs, values, practices, standards, language and stories—work discretely and together to maintain the dominant culture. This is the water in our gills and the air in our lungs, moving repetitiously through each of us every moment of every day. This repetitively reinforcing cycle is depicted in figure 1.

Figure 1. The culture cycle.

CULTURAL MYTHS

Culture and myth always go together. While the stories we tell ourselves reinforce the culture, there is often much in those stories that is more accurately termed myth. Myths, as defined next, are distinguished from mere stories by the varying levels of untruth, distortion or misinformation they contain.

A *myth* is a false story we tell ourselves to protect us from an uncomfortable truth, to prop up our withering ego, or to remind ourselves how special we are. Myths, in this sense, can reinforce the difference between "us" and "them" at the expense of truth. Often we are victims of our own stereotypes and shared myths, held captive to the worldview imposed onto us by the dominant culture. We don't see the way the cultural myth is shaping our thinking, feeling or behavior. Myths have some interesting characteristics that often reinforce the status quo culture.

Though they are part of the story we tell ourselves, myths are often *based on shared ignorance*. Consider the case of racism. It is often fueled by untrue caricatures of the stigmatized group. Cultural immersion—the exposure of an outsider to realities of other diverse cultures—has been shown to adversely affect the perpetuation of racism and ethnic stereotypes.. It's harder for us to judge those we come to know and appreciate. Racism does best where new thoughts about the out-group are kept away, allowing ignorance to persist.

Myths *operate outside of our awareness*. They typically continue because we don't identify their existence. They operate outside of our conscious thought and just seem to happen in or to us. Often, we don't realize we believe a myth until it asserts itself in our thinking in the midst of the experience it is related to. We don't recognize misogynist tendencies, for example, until we open our mouth in the midst of a discussion. "She was asking for it. Did you see the way she was dressed?" someone says of the woman victimized by rape, betraying his misunderstanding of the nature of rape. Myths hide until they are needed. When the situation dictates, they magically appear.[7]

Myths are *reinforced by the dominant culture*. Because myths tend to be things "everyone knows," we rarely question their content. We know them without thinking and more by osmosis as a part of our group's shared thinking. To question myths is to expose us to the possibility of ostracism from the group. It's much easier to go along with the crowd. We feel more than a tinge of discomfort when a coworker describes that "everyone starts from an equal opportunity in life." "They have the same opportunity to succeed or fail that I did," says the white, highly educated professional. We reinforce the myth with our silence.

Myths are *stubborn and resist change*. It's hard to change what we don't or won't see. We pretend we are color-blind or gender-blind or temperament-blind through our willful blindness.[8] It's hard to challenge things we know to be true, things we simply couldn't be wrong about, especially if we believe we don't have any biases. Human beings and especially human systems are highly resistant to change for this reason.

Lastly, myths are *highly contagious*. Everyone, almost without exception, is affected by myths. Even those who suffer because of them still tend to hold to and perpetuate them. Logically, it makes no sense to maintain a cultural myth about introversion. Yet, many of us knowingly or unknowingly perpetuate things about introversion, about ourselves, that aren't true. We are guilty of self-sabotage. We use sloppy language, describing ourselves as "shy" or "antisocial" rather than explaining how we are differently social and love people in an alternative way.

The culture is reinforced through the use of myths so those in power can remain in control. Those in power, though they are often not consciously aware of their biases, have a vested interest, nonetheless, in maintaining the perceived truth of myths about the out-groups. This is the nature of dominant culture.

DOMINANT CULTURE: POWER & POWERLESSNESS

The *dominant culture* is the particular cultural brand that is advanced and adhered to by those in power. In our original example, this was the white establishment in Los Angeles. The dominant culture is not always simply the *majority culture*, the numerical majority. It is reflected in and by the majority of people who breathe it in and out each day. These people may or may not be part of the dominant cultural group, but they assent to it anyway. In fact, a *vocal minority* often establishes the dominant culture of a group. Though it comprises less than half of the American culture, extroversion is a key aspect of our dominant culture in the West.[9]

Culture is always about *power*. The "in" group controls the cultural discussion, makes the rules, sets the standards, tells us what we should value, what we should believe, how we should live. Those who are outside of the in-group have limited choices. Either they aspire to the culture, values and norms of the in-group, or they are left with the only available options of forming their own subculture or, in extreme cases, overthrowing the dominant culture by means of revolution.

Dominant culture is not necessarily polite, especially in the West. It imposes itself upon us in and through the use of its mouthpiece, the media. Susan Cain warned us about "people who can't stop talking."[10] I would contend that we have an even greater foe in the media outlets, the magnified voices that do the bidding of the dominant culture. We are bombarded day in and day out with messages from Wall Street to Madison Avenue to Hollywood that tell us about the good of extroversion and the ills of introversion. The life of change, of taking risk, of breaking from the status quo is romanticized. Commercials abound reminding us of the problem of sadness and telling us of our right and need to be happy. The celebrities we idolize portray a life of constant pleasure, ease and luxury. Introverts are typically used as the antithesis, an example of what not to be.

I see the effects of this media bias when I work with groups of people. When I ask an audience how many consider themselves to be introverts, I rarely see anywhere near the number of hands go up that I know should be raised. Many are reticent to admit they are introverts. Only a few timid hands go up when it should be over half of the room, according to the demographic data.

The hesitancy of some to identify as introverts is a reflection of the perceived lack of power connected to that side of the equation. This is true of several aspects of power or powerlessness. Cultural power is found in various forms. These are the dimensions by which an individual within the culture finds advantages or disadvantages. There are at least seven key aspects or dimensions of power and privilege held by differing individuals:

1. Status: social, economic or both

2. Gender: maleness or femaleness

3. Ethnicity: racial or ethnic background, including primary language

4. Intelligences: IQ and other forms of positive intelligence differences

5. Temperament: various stable traits of personality (including introversion or extroversion)

6. Spirituality: perceived or professed connection to a higher power or to God

7. Attitude: how we choose to respond to life

Notice how many of these dimensions of power are unearned and simply part of being born into one category versus another. If an extroverted son with high natural intelligence happens to be born into an affluent, connected, white family, he has "won the lottery." He did nothing but be born, however, to deserve any of these five power dimensions. We appropriately refer to these serendipitous privileges as the "accidents of birth."[11]

I, myself, possess many of these unearned advantages in life, the notable exception being extroversion. If those of you who experience other dimensions of powerlessness were to judge my struggle as less significant than yours, I would not necessarily correct you. You may be tempted to say, "Get over it," to a white, middle-class male who has never experienced the pervasive and always present mistreatments or disadvantages of being female, non-white or poor. I wouldn't blame you for this sentiment.

Even if you have disadvantages greater than mine, there may also be another category to consider. In addition to your ethnicity, gender, socioeconomic status or other grounds for being treated as less-than, if you are reading this book, you are likely also introverted. These dimensions of powerlessness combine powerfully.

One of the most respected models of culture is that of Dutch psychologist Geert Hofstede. He has developed a six-component measurement of different cultures. One of his six dimensions is power, the degree to which members of a society accept the power imbalance as the acceptable status quo. In Hofstede's model, the United States has a score reflecting our moderate dissatisfaction with the way things are.[12] As a culture, we're not entirely comfortable with the imbalances around us related to the seven dimensions of power. This may be a vestige of our founding ideal that "all people are created equal," a romantic vision to which we aspire but that is difficult to live up to. Equality often comes with a price, especially on the part of those who currently hold dimensions of power in a society. Though many in our society are dissatisfied with the continued imbalance of power, few are willing to do the hard work required to change the situation.

Thinking about this power aspect of culture helps to understand the topic at hand, introversion, and why it shares some common ground with other disempowered people. As Susan Cain and others have argued, this new introvert movement is very similar to the civil rights or women's movements that have preceded it. If the problem in Watts in 1965 was powerlessness, a significant aspect of the current plight of introverts in the workplace and society at large is a more subtle, yet powerfully insidious, form of the same.

The dominant extrovert-biased culture in the West, *yang*, is the subject of the next chapter. For now, pause and reflect on the impact of culture on you as an introvert.

REFLECTION QUESTIONS

I became aware of the hidden power of culture somewhat later in life. Like Kevin the betta fish, I swam in the water for years and never paid much attention. Review these questions to explore your own experience with culture. Write your answers down, discuss them with a friend, or simply spend focused time thinking about your response.

1. How do you relate to Kevin? How has your culture impacted you positively? Negatively?

2. What beliefs or standards does your culture hold? Do you agree or disagree with those cultural beliefs? How does it enforce its standards?

3. What does your culture value? How are your personal values different?

4. How does the language of your culture reinforce its beliefs, values and standards? What words or phrases do the people

around you use to reinforce the beliefs, values and standards of your culture? How do people speak about introversion? How does that language affect you?

5. In what ways (dimensions of power) are you different from the dominant culture around you? How does this lack of power or privilege affect you?

6. As you begin this journey, on a scale of 1 to 10, how confident are you that you have what it takes to lead well as an introvert?

2

Yang

"American culture is CEO obsessed. We celebrate the hard-charging heroes and mythologize the iconoclastic visionaries. Those people are important."

**—Marcus Buckingham, best-selling author
and management expert**

In the summer of 1954, Joanne Schieble, a young graduate student at the University of Wisconsin, became pregnant. Her boyfriend, Abdul Fattah "John" Jandali, was a Syrian immigrant and fellow student at the university.[1] Schieble belonged to a white, conservative Christian family and could not convince her parents to allow her to marry a Muslim Arab.[2] The young mother saw no available option but to put the child she was carrying up for adoption. Her only requirement was that the child be adopted by two college graduates. The identified adoptive couple, an educated attorney and his college-educated wife, were scheduled to adopt the young boy but reneged at the last minute, preferring a girl instead. Joanne's boy was adopted by an uneducated couple living in San Francisco, California.

Their adopted son would never complete college, but would go on to become one of the most famously successful entrepreneurs of all time. Paul and Clara Jobs adopted their first son, Steve, at birth on February 24, 1955. Jobs, famous for his founding role of not only Apple Computer, but also NeXT and Pixar, epitomizes the *yang* leader. Driven and optimistic, at Apple he took the genius ideas of cofounder, Steve Wozniak, and parlayed the new inventions into a multibillion dollar business. Jobs leveraged his *yang* nature to win the hearts, minds and wallets of a generation.

For those who worked closely with Jobs, he was a driven and, at times, ruthless man. He was notoriously known as a fast-paced and out-of-the-box thinker. Wozniak said, in retrospect, that no one could contradict him. Jef Raskin, a key part of the Macintosh project, said of Jobs:

> He is a dreadful manager. . . . I have always liked Steve, I have found it impossible to work for him. . . . Jobs regularly misses appointments. . . . He acts without thinking and with bad judgment. . . . He does not give credit where due.[3]

His leadership style, for better and worse, made Apple what it became. Jobs, the man, was complicated. In addition to his extroverted traits, he also had a huge lack of sensitivity, often using his ability to read people and their vulnerabilities as a means of gaining advantage. He often used his charisma to manipulate people and was known as someone who struggled with telling the truth. Those who worked with him called this his "reality distortion field—a confounding mélange of a charismatic rhetorical style, indomitable will, and eagerness to bend any fact to fit the purpose at hand."[4]

Jobs was a driven, powerful, charismatic and larger-than-life figure obsessed with the creation of the types of products Apple has created.

I'm writing this book on an Apple computer. My laptop, and all of the other innovative Apple products, would not exist were it not for Steve Jobs's leadership in the field of technology. The ideas and inventions of Apple Computer have changed the world. *Yang* leaders are invaluable for being agents of this revolutionary kind of change.

YANG CULTURE

The world around us displays many examples of two things that exist in tension with one another in a way that makes life interesting. What would life be like without one side of important pairs: day and night, light and darkness, hot and cold, summer and winter, fast and slow, male and female? These complementary pairs have been viewed throughout human history in different ways.

In ancient Chinese philosophy, the world is seen as divided into these two opposite halves (*yin* and *yang*) needing balance (*he*, pronounced *huh?*). Chinese philosophy sees all of life as lived in between, or at the intersection of, *yin* and *yang*. Together, these "shape the holistic, dynamic and dialectical nature of culture."[5]

Yang represents "male" energy. It includes things such as sun, day, strength, brightness, hardness and masculinity.[6] It is the active side of life, creating room for the responses of *yin*. It is the approach side of life, benefitting from the receptivity of *yin*.

In people, *yang* involves activity. It, as a way of being, is less interested in contemplation and is always leaning toward results and experiences. It connects more readily to positive emotions. In particular, it seeks highly stimulating and pleasurable experiences that allow people to feel truly alive. It loves the thrill of victory and detests the agony of defeat. It struggles to understand the rationale for humility and naturally inclines toward positive self-regard. It loves risk, taking chances and being daring, and is less concerned about the boringness of safety. It lives in the moment and worries little about the future. It is a present and future-oriented optimism, in contrast to the pessimism that sometimes comes from dwelling on the past. It gets over things quickly and bounces back from adversity. Though it enjoys the company of others, ultimately it seeks the actualization of self and the joie de vivre that come from the journey. It celebrates its uniqueness and enjoys comparisons with others that highlight unique personal advantages. It is the mainstream of the American culture.

Yang is an outward orientation, prone toward experience and activity. It moves quickly and sometimes without adequate thoughtfulness or planning. It looks for adrenaline-promoting situations where winning is possible and loves the spotlight. It understands the debilitating effects of overly idealistic thinking and seeks instead to be fully present in what is. *Yang* is the dominant culture that we experience in the West. Extroversion is *yang*.

DISC & EXTROVERSION

Different models for understanding human behavior have been proposed. As George Box famously said, "All models are wrong but some are useful."[7] One widely used model for understanding people and their behavior is the DISC model. I have found this model provides a helpful and nuanced understanding of each person's place on the introvert-extrovert continuum. Because of this, I use DISC as my primary means of helping clients better understand who they are in relation to this important aspect of self. To read more of the how and why I use DISC to help clients understand not only their introversion or extroversion, but its specific type, see Appendix A: Measuring Introversion-Extroversion with DISC. You can also learn more about the specific DISC assessment I use by going to http://ttisuccessinsights.com/how/five-sciences /behaviorsdisc.

The DISC helps to identify extroversion. Extroversion is the preferred temperament in Western culture. In the United States, we tend to promote the ideal of leadership as a combination of a can-do, results orientation and visionary, optimistic, or even charismatic traits.

There is a great deal of misunderstanding related to the concepts of introversion and extroversion in our culture. It is critical that we better understand these constructs; to help, here is my definition of extroversion (I'll define introversion in the next chapter):

Extroversion is a fast-paced, outward-oriented, stimulus-seeking trait that affects an individual's thinking, feeling and behavior.

Most assessments of personality or temperament only give an overall score related to introversion or extroversion. The DISC model breaks introversion and extroversion into two distinct, yet interrelated, halves. Within extroversion, there is a distinction between task orientation (represented by "D" in DISC) and people orientation (represented by "I"); together, those two halves make up our understanding of extroversion as a whole (see figure 2). The D can stand for "dominant" and the I for "influencing."

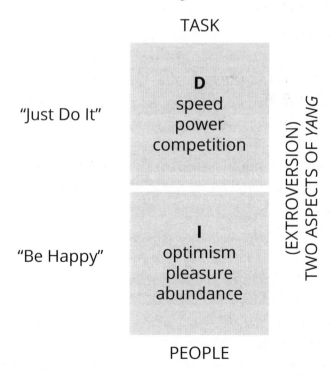

Figure 2. The two *yang* components of extroversion.

We begin our exploration of extroversion on the task side with high-D extroversion.

JUST DO IT (HIGH-D EXTROVERSION)

In 1976, Gary Gilmore killed two people in Utah. Just before he was executed by a firing squad, his famous last words were, "Let's do it." A little over a decade later, Portland ad man Dan Wieden picked up Gilmore's haunting words and modified them to create one of the best known slogans in history. Shirts with the motto, "Just do it," can be found in remote villages all over the world. The slogan, the shoes and apparel that go with it have spread the message of the United States abroad.

In America, we value results. "Talk is cheap," we say. What matters most to us is the outcome. Now, thanks to Nike, the whole world believes we Americans believe in "just do it."

One of the most common cultural myths in the West is, "You are what you do." When we meet someone, we ask them, "What do you do?" This is a *yang* question. In *yin* cultures, the question is instead, "Who are you?" The "just do it" aspect of *yang* culture emphasizes action over being. It is a task-oriented expression of *yang* values. It is driven for results and will settle for nothing less than winning. It has a hard time, however, relaxing, often failing to enjoy the spoils it collects. There are at least three noteworthy aspects of this task side of *yang* culture.

High-D extroversion is about *speed*. The United States is an immediate-gratification culture. We don't just value results; we value the immediacy of those results. We want what we want and we want it now. Fast is never fast enough. We are constantly seeking to accomplish and obtain things in a faster way. This is often the attitude in the workplace. Immediate results are often preferred over the superior results that might come from longer, slower (even healthier) processes. Time is money. Time is wasting. *Yang* people keep things moving toward the goal.

High-D extroversion is also about *power*. Just like Steve Jobs, other yang leaders and cultures know what they want and will use the means at their disposal to get it. *Yang* is driven and can be dominating. It is not for the faint or the weak and tends to have a measure of intolerance or disdain for such kinds of people. In some ways, it is similar to social Darwinism, an idea that became popular in the American culture in the 1870s. Social Darwinism suggests that society would benefit from the elimination of the weak by means of natural selection and survival of the fittest. It can be a very win-lose orientation. It inevitably uses power, whether for good or ill ends. Power, in healthy *yang* people, is leveraged for the sake of achieving a higher good. In other less healthy individuals, it can be used to get results at the expense of people in the way.

Thirdly, high-D extroversion is *competitive*. It is about bottom line, results, profitability and success. We celebrate champions in the realms of sports, business and all walks of life. We have license plates that read, "He who dies with the most toys wins." You won't see those in the East. We have a whole state in the Union, Texas, dedicated to the goodness of bigness. In the United States, we tend to equate bigger with better. Large companies are seen as success stories. If a company or organization remains small, we worry that something is wrong. Often the means to this growth are aggressive. Competing is part of life and a necessary part of survival. *Yang*-oriented people keep us focused on the prize, the results.

Not surprisingly, the dominant emotion usually associated with this aspect of *yang* is anger. It is a short-fused temper that can quickly escalate and just as quickly dissipate. This anger at others is often a symptom of holding others to a high standard, but giving oneself a pass. Sometimes, this aspect of *yang* resembles the motto, "Do as I say, not as I do." Seeing the world as inherently competitive, high-D people often report they have a strong fear of being taken advantage of. This fear may arise, in some cases, as they reflect on the possibility of others using tactics to win that are similar to their own.

In any case, this aspect of leadership is needed to move teams toward greater results, higher profits and greater efficiency and accomplish all of this with greater speed. It is the orientation we need most in times of crisis, where quick, decisive direction is needed.

High-D, task-oriented extroversion is only half of the *yang* side of the equation. There is also the people-oriented aspect. This high-I type of extroversion is most likely the one we think of when we hear the word extrovert used in popular conversation. Most of the time, the term is used to apply to someone who is optimistic and outgoing, a "happy" person.

BE HAPPY (HIGH-I EXTROVERSION)

Pharrell Williams's song, "Happy," resonates in our society. Before that, "Don't Worry, Be Happy" put Bobby McFerrin at the top of the charts. Western culture, some have argued, is increasingly happiness obsessed. In 2000, there were fifty books written promoting the good of happiness listed on Amazon. In 2008, that number had grown to four thousand.[8] *Yang* culture is not only about getting things done, it's also about a particular kind of happiness, "feeling good."

Happiness, in America, is our understood birthright. We can and should be happy.[9] In fact, if people aren't happy enough, we worry and quickly send them off to physicians or mental health practitioners who will prescribe sufficient doses of "happy pills" to remedy the situation.[10]

From the sixties and seventies forward, our previously "repressed" culture has held to a notion that says, "If it feels good, do it." This adage suggests that personal pleasure (*hedonism*) is the ultimate principle. Feeling good, having pleasure, this is the *yang* idea of happiness in Western culture. This cultural obsession is often spurred on by a related preference for materialism, believing that more things will make us happy. Ironically, the pursuit of happiness has left us terribly unhappy.[11] It seems that the harder we pursue happiness, the less we experience it. Yet, we persist in our relentless pursuit. Happiness is the people and experiential side of *yang*. It can also be broken down into three main aspects.

High-I extroversion is eternally *optimistic*. It cannot help but see the glass as half full. When it encounters adversity, it perseveres like little orphan Annie, in large part, due to a belief that tomorrow will be better than today. *Yang*-oriented, people-focused individuals tend to align with the teachings of positive psychology, which suggests that we can create good results through the power of positive thinking.[12] This message of positivity has permeated our culture and greatly influenced all aspects of our society, from work, to school, to religious organizations. Its ability to deliver on its promise remains to be seen. Optimism, in appropriate doses, is necessary in society. People-oriented extroverts bring the vision and hope people need to keep moving toward the future.

High-I extroversion is also about *pleasure*, feeling good and having fun. This fun is the reward that comes to those who win using the power side of *yang*. Happiness, then, is derivative because it is drawn from positive life experiences. Positive emotions are emphasized. There is no room for negative feelings like anxiety or sadness. "Life is short," our culture says. "Play hard." *Yang* people remind us of the importance of joy in the journey. Life is short and many of us benefit from the positive impact of the fun created by *yang* people around us.

High-I extroversion is thirdly about *abundance*. Quantity is more important than quality. More is better. We should not only be happy and optimistic, we should expect things to come our way in large quantities. We are a culture of "never enough."[13] This perceived scarcity may be connected to an unhealthy sense of entitlement. As a culture, we feel as if we each deserve the best things life has to offer. For this problem, *yang* philosophy offers a solution, the power of positive thinking leading to a life of prosperity. America has truly been one of the most prosperous civilizations in history. We have much to be thankful for and owe much of that to the contribution of *yang*-oriented people all around us.

High-I leadership is needed for the sake of continuing hope, vision and optimism. These are the dreamers who help all of us think about what could be. They are the ones who help us laugh and take ourselves less seriously sometimes. They continue to expand the limits of our relational network by connecting us with new people. For these reasons, we need them on our teams and in leadership roles.

Like Steve Jobs, many extroverts, both high-D and high-I, tend to see life through a more individualistic lens. Their focus is on themselves, their uniqueness, the way they stand out from the crowd. They connect with the "me" culture around us.

IT'S ABOUT "ME": THE INDEPENDENT SELF

Yang culture has one more characteristic or abiding trait, its *independent* orientation. In a recent ad campaign for Korean Airlines in the U.S. market, the slogan reads, "It's all about you." For years, Burger King, an American icon, told us to "have it your way."

Yang, the dominant culture in the United States and exported abroad, is about the *individual*. On the Hofstede cultural scale, we Americans have almost a perfect score on the individualism dimension, reflecting our incredibly strong *yang* bias.[14] Hofstede described an individualistic society as one "in which the ties between individuals are loose; everyone is expected to look after himself or herself and his or her immediate family."[15] It's about looking out for number one.

Though many extroverts enjoy large crowds, socializing, and building vast networks of social or business contacts, at their root, extroverts tends to be more independent. It is a more outward focus for the individual as he or she seeks results or happiness in the world. Relationships with others often have a self-oriented focus.

Hazel Markus, the social psychologist introduced earlier, and her colleague Shinobu Kitayama wrote a seminal article in 1991 describing the different ways people see themselves according to the different cultural contexts they find themselves in.[16] In the West, people are seen as independent, self-contained, autonomous individuals who embody a unique set of internal attributes (traits, abilities, motives, values) and who behave primarily according to those attributes. This is the culture of "me."

For example, we tend in the West to default to understanding people as creators of their destiny, captains of their ships, rather than seeing them as limited by their context. The emphasis falls metaphorically on the fish. What kind of a fish is Kevin? What traits does he have or lack that explain his behavior? If something is wrong, we look to the individual as the reason and the source of the dysfunction. The emphasis is not on the water in the bowl, the cultural or environmental factors that help explain the situation. For those who do well, the credit goes to the individual. "Kevin is just a better fish." For those who don't, the blame. "Kevin is just a bad fish." In neither case is the environment given much credit in relation to the outcome. It's not about the water or the fishbowl. The individual is seen as autonomous, acting alone and responsible for his or her own success or failure.

This focus on the individual and an independent sense of well-being or happiness means *yang*-oriented people tend to most fear any form of social rejection that will be experienced as unhappiness. The stress is on uniqueness, the need to individuate,[17] and an appreciation for individual strengths as differentiators from the crowd.[18] The West also emphasizes asserting oneself in order to get what one needs or wants out of life. Passivity is frowned upon as an unhealthy attribute. All of these point to a connection between *yang* culture, extroversion, and the *independent self.* That independent self connects to a way of thinking about the good life.

THE GOOD LIFE: *HEDONIA*

Throughout history, mankind has been engaged in a conversation about what constitutes "the good life." In the fifth century BCE, the Greek playwright Sophocles said that the chief element of happiness is wisdom. A century later, Aristotle famously coined the phrase "the good life" (*eudaimonia*) referring to our highest good or happiness.

In his 2013 book, *The Good Life: What Makes a Life Worth Living?*, Hugh McKay explored the ways in which Western *yang* culture has modified Aristotle's original ideals to fit its current paradigm. *Yang* culture says work should be fun, marriage should be fun, everything should be fun. We should all win; losing has no place. McKay called all of this "the utopia complex." Utopians "are conditioned (and are busily conditioning their children) to assume that perfection in anything should be within their grasp."[19]

McKay quoted Richard Eckersley, an Australian social analyst, who bemoaned this redefinition of the good life:

A cultural focus on the external trappings of "the good life" increases the pressures to meet high, even unrealistic, expectations and so heightens the risks of failure and disappointment. It leads to an unrelenting need to make the most of one's life, to fashion identity and meaning increasingly from personal achievements and possessions and less from shared cultural traditions and beliefs. It distracts people from what is most important to well-being: the quality of their relationships.[20]

The good life is a life of abundance, happiness and success. It's full of pleasure, comfort and ease. It's fun. It is a life filled with positive emotions and devoid of negative ones. The ancient Greeks gave us a word for this, *hedonia*, from which we derive the word hedonism. The good life = independence + happiness (pleasure resulting from more stuff and fun experiences) + results (success resulting from our driven, winner-take-all attitude and competitiveness). This *yang* definition of the good life has become the more recent understanding of the American dream, which some have suggested may be the American nightmare.[21]

REFLECTION QUESTIONS

Yang culture is the dominant culture in the West. Thinking about the culture you swim in, consider the following questions.

1. What do you think about the leadership of Steve Jobs? Could he have gotten the results he obtained if he were less of a *yang* leader?

2. Why do we need *yang* in our society?

3. What parts of *yang* culture are most difficult for you? Personally? Professionally?

4. What positive myths about extroversion bother you most?

5. As you compare yourself to the standard of *yang* culture, how do you fare?

    a. On speed? Do you go "too slow" and get run over sometimes?

    b. On power? Are you a "power" person, or do you lead others differently?

    c. On competitiveness? How assertive are you? Must you win?

    d. On optimism? Do you see the glass as half full?

    e. On happiness? Are you happy enough?

    f. On quantity over quality? Are you driven to have more?

    g. On being independent, me-oriented? Do you tend to focus on self or others?

6. Are you living the "good life," as defined by *yang* culture?

Yin

"Life doesn't make any sense without interdependence. We need each other, and the sooner we learn that, the better for us all."

—Erik Erikson

On August 11, 1950, fifteen years to the day before the beginning of the riots in Watts and my birthday, a male child was born to a couple in Sunnyvale, California. His father, Jerry, had a knack for putting things together and an interest in electronics. Steve, the firstborn in his family, followed in his father's footsteps and was similarly gifted at assembling things. He loved Tom Swift books, which focused on great adventures. As an adolescent, Steve entered the junior high science fair with a homemade computer of sorts that played tic-tac-toe. He enjoyed learning from his teacher, John MacCallum, who also led the electronics club at school. Steve was an awkwardly social young man who never had a date, let alone a girlfriend, during high school. He was, however, an expert prankster.

When Steve graduated from high school, he went off to the University of Colorado. His first semester, he lived in the freshman dorm. Steve soon lost interest in college life and moved home to attend De Anza Community College for the remainder of the year. In the fall, he enrolled at UC Berkeley where he would soon meet not only Captain Crunch, the eventual inventor of the first blue box, but also another young entrepreneur he would eventually partner with to change the world, in the context of the Home Brew Computer Club.

Famously, Steve created the first version of the Atari game "Breakout." His friend, a fellow Home Brew member and neighbor, had asked him to create the software in only four days, and then took more than fifty percent of the bonus they received from Atari for the project. Who was this neighbor and friend? The young entrepreneur, Steve Jobs. This creative genius game designer was Steve Wozniak. The Jobs-Wozniak tandem would go on to collaborate on the first personal computers as part of a small, unknown, start-up company known as Apple Computer.

Wozniak, "Woz," typifies the quiet leader, the *yin* side of the equation. His attention to detail and deep loyalty to both people and causes are typical of *yin* leaders. For Wozniak, his dedication to Jobs was key to the success and creativity of Apple. Wozniak's sense of loyalty extended beyond Jobs and Apple. Many are not aware of Wozniak's commitment to the US Festival, an event started by Woz with the help of the famous concert promoter, Bill Graham. As a reaction to the "Me generation" of the 70s, Steve wanted to start a community-minded event that was more about "us." The first US Festival event was held at Glen Helen Regional Park in Devore, California, in the fall of 1982. Woz's commitment to Jobs and to the US Festival typifies the loyalty and group-orientation in *yin* leaders.

Woz normally preferred to work behind the scenes, even being the comedic voice on the other end of the phone on the "Dial-a-Joke" line he created. Wozniak distinguished himself from Steve Jobs:

> Steve's [Jobs'] contributions could have been made without so many stories about him terrorizing folks. I like being more patient and not having so many conflicts. I think a company can be a good family. If the Macintosh project had been run my way, things probably would have been a mess. But I think if it had been a mix of both our styles, it would have been better than just the way Steve [Jobs] did it.[1]

Wozniak and Jobs were a perfect *yin* and *yang* partnership. Woz was the real brains of the operation who liked to work creatively behind the scenes. Jobs, on the other hand, liked being the visible leader. Together, they accomplished things neither could likely have accomplished alone.

YIN CULTURE

Steve Jobs is to *yang* as Wozniak is to *yin*. Without Jobs' active promotion and marketing, the ideas and inventions of Steve Wozniak might never have led to a personal computing revolution. *Yin* needs *yang*; it acts in response to *yang*. This need for the other, *interdependence*, is a characteristic of this side, the *yin* side, of the cultural equation.

In ancient Chinese philosophy, *yin* represents "female" energy. It includes things such as moon, night, weakness, darkness, softness and femininity.[2] It is the reactive side of life, responding to the actions of *yang*. It is the receptive side of life, responding to the movements of *yang*. The tide moves in (*yang*) and out (*yin*). The waves rise (*yang*), crash and diminish (*yin*) on the shore. All the while, the sea represents the *yin* side of life, exerting a calming effect on many who seek the solace of the shore.

Yin involves the reflective and contemplative side of being human. It causes us to seek higher degrees of meaning, to search after the larger purpose of our existence. It is more existential. It connects more readily to many of the emotions commonly called "negative." It feels sadness deeply and has a natural tendency toward empathy, especially feeling the sadness of others. It is intuitively connected less with victory and more with fear. It naturally feels humility and struggles less with pride. It tends to avoid risk and prefer safety. The combination of fear-proneness and sadness make it slow and halting toward anger and aggression. It has a long, patient fuse. Because it is so naturally about seeking to preserve harmony and peace among a family or group, *yin* seeks to smooth over the rough spots in relationships, even at its own expense. It feels deep loyalty to the group, the causes and the people to whom it connects.

It is a more inward inclination, prone toward self-awareness, for better or worse. It thinks deeply and moves more slowly and deliberately. It searches for truth, goodness and beauty in the world and has a hard time settling for lesser forms of any of these. In other words, it has high standards. It understands and longs for justice and equity, for a sense of things being as they ought to be. *Yin* is the dominant culture in the East. Introversion is *yin*.

DISC & INTROVERSION

The DISC also helps us identify introversion. Introversion, though the preferred temperament in the East, is often viewed negatively in the West. Because there is so much misunderstanding, it is helpful to define introversion. Here is my definition of this trait of individual temperament:

Introversion is a slower-paced, inward-oriented, stimulus-averse trait that affects an individual's thinking, feeling and behavior.

The DISC model helps us see the two sides of introversion. In a sense, there are two distinct kinds of introversion that together make the whole of this aspect of temperament. Some of us have a more people-oriented (represented by "S" in DISC) form of introversion and others have a more task-oriented (represented by "C") introverted temperament. You can see these two aspects of introversion and how they fit together in figure 3.

Figure 3. The two *yin* components of introversion.

Starting on the people side of introversion, notice the characteristics of a high-S behavioral style.

THINK ABOUT IT (HIGH-S INTROVERSION)

Though plenty of introverts wear Nike, *yin* culture is philosophically opposed to the mind-set that says, "Just do it." It doesn't fit as well on a T-shirt, but its slogan would be, "Don't just do it; think about it." It tends to be more careful, cautious and thoughtful. It prizes wisdom above decisiveness, logic above hype, and reason over emotion. This side of *yin* is focused on people and tends to calculate the impact on a group of actions or decisions. For this reason, it is somewhat averse to change, especially the sort that causes unnecessary disruption or distress among a group. By this same logic, it prefers steadiness and stability, seeing value in leaving things that aren't broken alone. There are three aspects of this people-oriented *yin* behavior.

High-S introversion is about *carefulness*, creating safety by moving cautiously. It moves more slowly and has an aversion to risk built into its nature. Wisdom is often connected to prudence and the exercise of appropriate caution. It rightly questions taking risks that could prove to damage a group. It intuitively senses the potential harm that could come to team members through the implementation of a poorly conceived plan or unhealthy group dynamics. When pushed by more *yang*-oriented people, *yin* will tend to dig in and resist being prematurely driven to a solution, being sometimes seen as stubborn. Stubbornness, though, is often merely loyalty differently understood. Loyalty involves sticking with a person, cause or idea, even in the face of adversity or needed change. Many extroverts are frustrated by this aspect of *yin*-oriented introversion that seems to hinder progress and slow things down.

Secondly, high-S introversion is about others, about *deference* to them. *Yin* culture tends to emphasize others over self. Today, the S in DISC is normally connected to "steadiness." In Marston's original model, the S stood for "submission."[3] Submission is not normally praised in Western culture today. Maturity for high-S introverts is seen more in terms of humility and servanthood than it is in terms of self-actualization or ego strength. This aspect of *yin* is about the team, the group, the whole rather than the individual. It sees the group as family and has corresponding familial-type loyalty. This explains why *yin* people are usually the ones holding the team together like glue. It holds self to a high standard and for the sake of the team and loyalty can tend to give others a pass. For this reason, *yin* can result in unhealthy, lose-win relationships, especially with *yang*-oriented people.

While *yin* people feel various emotions in the course of their interactions with others, they tend to suppress those emotions, to self-censor what they are feeling for the sake of the team. "It's not important. I'm fine," they'll reason. These are worn-out phrases for this kind of introvert who tends to value others as more important than self. Constantly deferring to others can over time turn them into doormats, people others wipe their feet on. This is an aspect of high-S introversion that requires good self-awareness and management for *yin* people.

Lastly, high-S introversion is about *logic*. *Yin* is about wisdom, the use of deep thought and reason in a logical fashion to gain greater understanding. It smells out the improper use of emotion and subjectivity being used as mere hype, spin or propaganda. In this way, it is highly sensitive to potential manipulation as if it has a built-in lie detector. It seeks after carefully thought-through, proven solutions to problems and has the patience to work toward that end.

Organizations of all kinds need high-S introverted leadership. The natural inclination toward the team and a healthy aversion to unnecessary risk that could harm the team balances the *yang* side of the leadership equation. The calm, steady, composed and logical approach to decision making is needed to continue to create safety and stability for the group.

The high-S, people-oriented kind of introversion is only half of the *yin* side of life. Introversion also includes a task orientation that constantly pushes the team and the self toward greater degrees of quality and "rightness."

DO IT RIGHT (HIGH-C INTROVERSION)

On the task side, *yin* culture is less about personal happiness and more about truth and doing what is right and in the best interest of everyone. Like Jack Webb in *Dragnet*, it seeks "just the facts, ma'am." It moves more slowly, seeking the collection of all the data before a decision is made. It is driven, yet in a different way than *yang*. This drivenness is toward perfection, quality and high standards rather than quick results. It cares just as much about the means as it does the ends. Things need to be done right. There are three aspects of task-oriented *yin* that can be readily observed.

High-C introversion is about *realism*, as opposed to the sometimes unrealistic optimism of *yang*. At times, reality can be harsh and hard to face. *Yin* culture values facing hard realities, including those we would much rather gloss over, as opposed to the denial and unfounded optimism that sometimes prevails in *yang* culture. Its realism is often perceived by *yang* individuals as pessimism. Whatever it is called, it is an innate ability to poke holes in ill-conceived plans or ideas that characterizes this aspect of *yin*. Physician, psychologist and social activist Havelock Ellis reflected the bias of *yin* culture when he commented, "The place where optimism most flourishes is the lunatic asylum."[4]

Yin culture does not tend toward entitlement like *yang*, but to the opposite. It can be a somewhat deprecating culture that fails to recognize the rights or achievements of the individual. There can be a "you deserve nothing" sort of pessimistic outlook within a cultural context of duty. In contrast to the power or success orientation of *yang*, *yin* can hold to the opposite principle of minimalism, believing that less is more. This can be either healthy or not.

Consistent with a sober approach to life that faces reality, high-C introversion is secondly about seeking *meaning*. In this way, it opposes the happy-go-lucky approach to life. *Yin* life is more than shallow happiness. It is about trying to change the brokenness in the world, the many things that aren't right. Because the world around us is confusing and filled with so much pain, the *yin* way of life is often protesting the injustices, the oppression, and the suffering. It is this ability to see the problems that gives *yin* a reputation with *yang* of being "too serious" or "too sad."

High-C introversion is lastly about *rightness*, compliance with an external standard or expectation. In fact, the "C" in DISC often stands for "compliance." This also includes a strong desire for quality as more important than quantity. Doing things right is more important than getting things done. There is no point in claiming to have finished a project that still contains errors. This incessant focus on quality often exacerbates the impatience of *yang*.

Believing that rightness is superior, *yin* culture sometimes professes that life is about pain and suffering as a martyr for the truth, as opposed to shallowly pursuing happiness. It sometimes similarly believes that what feels good should be avoided, as reflected in various forms of asceticism, the idea that good people ought to forego earthly pleasures for the sake of becoming mature.

Its ideals are standards to which it holds individuals very responsible. It relentlessly pursues perfection, particularly in its own work product, but also in its moral and ethical life. It tends to be generally hard on all people, self included, expecting everyone to achieve high-ethical and high-quality results in the workplace. The dominant emotion connected with this aspect of *yin* is fear, fear of making mistakes, fear of errors, fear of imperfection, fear of not doing things "right."

Both sides of introversion, high S and high C, have a different orientation than extroversion. *Yang* culture emphasizes the individual. *Yin* culture emphasizes the group.

IT'S ABOUT "US": THE INTERDEPENDENT SELF

Steve Wozniak created the US Festival as a way to counter what he perceived to be the negative effects of the Me generation he was part of in the 70s.[5] The festival was described to prospective participating rock bands as the opposite of Woodstock, a gathering that would be focused on the one world of which we are all a part. The event was connected via satellite links to the then-present Soviet Union. Moving from "me" to "us" was a societal change Steve Wozniak was willing to invest $13 million of his own money in, eventually losing an estimated $20 million, to help bring to fruition. This group mind-set and collectivistic passion in Wozniak are important and noteworthy aspects of *yin* culture.

Yin culture is not about the individual; it's about the group. It is a collective mind-set. The focus is on *us*, how *we* can make meaning together. In fact, in an Eastern *yin* mind-set, the individual cannot really understand himself or herself in isolation from the group. When you meet someone from the East, the first question is not, "What do you do?" but "Who are you?" The meaning: Which family are you a part of? How are you connected in terms of family ties? This thinking is completely foreign to us in the West.

Markus and Kitayama, the social psychologists we met in the last chapter, distinguished between the *yang* independent self and the *yin* interdependent self.[6] Whereas *yang* tends to be shaped by attending to self, appreciating and emphasizing differences, and self-assertiveness, the *yin* picture is the opposite. The *interdependent self* is focused on attending to others, thinking about the impact of one's actions on the group. It is characterized by a desire to fit or blend in as opposed to standing out. It remains focused on group well-being, seeking a sense of harmonious interdependence between group members, even at the expense of the self. It is the culture of "we."

Several *yin* cultural myths connect to this aspect of interdependence. In *yin* cultures, the group is not only valued as more important than the individual but sometimes at the expense of the individual. For instance, it is widely understood that Asian cultures tend to be known as honor cultures. In an honor culture, the acts of the individual reflect on the entire extended family, either bringing honor or shame. These Asian cultures tend to view the individualistic, loud, obnoxious extrovert that travels abroad as an example of the ugly American. These cultures often see American relationships as egocentric and off-puttingly shallow.

Similar to how introversion is often seen as a choice in Western culture, extroversion can also be seen as a choice in Eastern culture. Extroverted individuals in Scandinavia or Asia, *yin*-dominant cultures, can be encouraged to behave like introverts, rather than the extroverts they are.

Being oneself is a major theme of this book. Whatever your disposition, living and leading as your true self are keys to the good life.

THE GOOD LIFE: *EUDAIMONIA*

Sophocles and Aristotle began the discussion of the "good life" almost twenty-five hundred years ago. Aristotle used the word happiness, *eudaimonia*, in the original Greek, in his writings. But since the time of Aristotle, and particularly in recent decades, the word happiness has been hijacked to mean something entirely different than what the likely introverted Aristotle intended.

Aristotle's concept of ultimate happiness, *eudaimonia*, has to do with striving after purpose, meaning and fulfillment as opposed to pleasure, joy or blind optimism. Happiness is found in fulfilling the ultimate purpose for which we exist, our why. This why is intrinsically connected to our vision of the world as it should be. Simon Sinek, a *yin* thought leader, described two things all leaders must have: a vision of the world that does not exist and the ability to communicate it.[7]

What is the good life in *yin* culture? In contrast to the happiness, success or pleasure of the *yang* culture, *yin* looks to alternative measures of goodness. In a *yin* world, satisfaction, meaning, truth and beauty all combine to form the ideal. The good life is the life lived in pursuit of what matters, a why significant enough to sustain our efforts at change and growth over the course of a lifetime.

REFLECTION QUESTIONS

If you had been born in Asia or Scandinavia, your cultural experiences as an introvert may have been quite different. You may not have become a "rock star," but the metaphor may have been fitting, nonetheless. You might have stood out as your natural self in a positive way. As you reflect on the following, think about *yin* culture and its impact on you:

1. How did Steve Wozniak need Steve Jobs to help transform his ideas into reality? Without Wozniak, would Steve Jobs have accomplished what he did?

2. Why do we need *yin* in our society? *Yin* leaders? You?

3. What would a *yang*-only society look like? A *yin*-only society? What would be missing?

4. As you compare yourself to the *yin* cultural standard, how do you fare?

    a. On carefulness and caution? Do you believe in the avoidance of unnecessary risk?

    b. On deference to others? Should others be considered equal to or better than you?

    c. On logic and reason? Are you wary of emotional appeals?

d. On being realistic (pessimistic)? Can you see problems in plans and schemes? Is this a strength?

e. On pursuing meaning? Do you value purpose over fun?

f. On being compliant, seeking truth? How much does doing the right thing matter to you?

g. On being interdependent, we-oriented? Do you tend to focus on others or yourself?

5. How would you define the good life?

And

"The rapprochement of peoples is only possible when differences of culture and outlook are respected and appreciated rather than feared and condemned, when the common bond of human dignity is recognized as the essential bond for a peaceful world."

—J. William Fulbright

The year was 1776. The War for Independence, sometimes known as the American Revolution, had already begun. The Continental Congress convened in Philadelphia primarily to draft the document that would explain the rationale for the revolution. The document would focus first and foremost on the problem of King George III of England, who had at least three significant problems as a leader:

- The problem of abstraction: treating people like things. Simon Sinek recently pointed out this tendency that seems to recur throughout human history.[1] At various times and for various reasons, people in power, "positional leaders," begin to lose touch with those they "lead." Instead of serving them and influencing them in healthy ways, their leadership becomes about them, the "leaders." The people "below" them become numbers, rather than real people who matter, with real lives and families. George was so disconnected across the pond from the colonies; they had become mere abstractions to him.

- The problem of positional-only leadership: pulling rank. Some leaders are all about their titles. There is hardly any title that wields more power than the word "king." Perhaps this went to George's head. His leadership was completely separated from those he led. He definitely did not identify as one of them, but rather as a rank above them, a position given, in his mind, by no less than God Himself.

- The problem of flying solo: leading in isolation. George was notoriously known for not listening to his counselors. He most certainly was warned about the detrimental effect of his over-taxation policies on the colonists. His advisors advised. He ignored them all and stayed the course. Just like Frank Sinatra, he did it "his way."

Of these three *yang*-related problems that George had, the last is perhaps the one at the forefront of the colonial minds gathered in Philadelphia that July. They were about to undertake the birth of a new nation, a new society. How would they govern themselves? How would they avoid the problems that inevitably come from solitary leadership? How would they make sure that no George (neither George III nor George Washington) would become a dictator?

George III, some have argued, was one of the worst leaders in history. His failed leadership, consistent with the policies of those who preceded him, motivated the colonists to create a new form of government that would be the opposite of George's solo monarchy. Beginning that July and continuing over the next few decades, the leaders of this new nation began to articulate a new form of government, one based on *balance*. Three branches would keep each other in check. No one person or branch would have all the power, but all would share leadership in a harmonious fashion. The new government would involve many leaders from *we the people*, bringing their unique strengths and perspectives to bear on the decisions that would shape this new nation. This can be seen as an unprecedented, historical and continuing experiment in leadership.

BALANCE (*HE*)

It's been over two hundred years since this nation was founded. The American experiment continues. At the beginning of the twenty-first century, humans find themselves with an ever-increasing intolerance for ambiguity and uncertainty. In a world that feels always expanding and increasingly complex, we look for anything to give us greater security in the form of absolutes. Division, however, is everywhere. We are deeply divided politically, ideologically, religiously, ethnically, by gender and in countless other ways. We live and breathe either-or thinking.

Several years ago, Jim Collins and Jerry Porras suggested in their book *Built to Last* that great organizations don't allow themselves to become caught up in either-or thinking. Here's how they expressed the nature of healthy and visionary companies:

Instead of being oppressed by the "Tyranny of the OR," highly visionary companies liberate themselves with the "Genius of the AND"—the ability to embrace both extremes of a number of dimensions at the same time. Instead of choosing between A *OR* B, they figure out a way to have both A *AND* B.[2]

They went on to articulate a dynamic interdependence between what are described in this book as *yin* and *yang* aspects of organizational behavior. What they did not explicitly connect was the varied yet complementary kinds of temperaments, ranging from introverted to extroverted, in different leaders around the executive table. This combination of different individual traits would have served as a better model than the solo leadership of George III.

The document the Congress created in 1776 was titled the Declaration of Independence. Initially, it was clearly meant to be independence from England and George's tyranny. However, that first step toward independence led to the creation of a culture perhaps overly marked by that trait. In distinction from other more interdependent cultures, American culture has been on a steady march toward hyper-independence and its related ideas of individuation and autonomy.

In chapter two, the idea was introduced from ancient Eastern philosophy that the proper balance of *yin* and *yang* results in *he*. *He* is often translated from Chinese as "peace." For most Americans, our concept of peace reflects an "absence of conflict." In other words, peace means we're taking a break from killing each other. This only loosely connects to the real meaning of *he*. *He* is better translated "completeness," "wholeness" or "harmoniousness."[3]

The world around us cries out for this kind of balance and wholeness. Male and female, hot and cold, summer and winter stand in contrast, despite the implied need for the other. The world around us is diverse. And yet, so often, we organize as subcultures around one side of the whole and seek after conformity with only half of the equation. This never ends well.

Instead, a world of *he* is a world that holds diverse things in harmony together. It doesn't prefer *yin* or *yang* but holds *yin* and *yang* in careful balance. Tony Fang, a business professor at Stockholm University, nicely summed up the need for a *yin yang* approach:

The Yin Yang suggests that human beings, organizations, and cultures, like all other universal phenomena, intrinsically crave variation and harmony for their sheer existence and healthy development. We are "both/and" instead of "either/or." We are both Yin and Yang, feminine and masculine, long-term and short-term, individualistic and collectivistic, . . . depending on situations, context and time.[4]

When it comes to professional life and leadership, the both-and world of balance described by *he* includes two important aspects: you and the leadership team in your organization

A BALANCED YOU

Not only is the world balanced, or seeking balance, you as an individual also have a need for this balance. This is intrapersonal *he*, a healthy recognition of not only the way you connect with those around you in healthy interdependence but also the way you are uniquely and independently you. Reid Hoffman, the introverted founder of LinkedIn, had a great phrase to describe this reality. He called this I to the We: I^{we}. Hoffman explained that "An individual's power is raised exponentially with the help of a team (a network). But just as zero to the one hundredth power is still zero, there's no team without the individual."[5]

It's not an either-or but a both-and. The team needs the individual strengths you bring, and you wouldn't be able to leverage those strengths for maximum benefit without the team on which you depend.

You'll notice that the *yin yang* symbol illustrates a drop of each in the other. In other words, you have some of each. A healthy self involves aspects of both your *yin* (collective) self and your *yang* (individual) self. Healthy people, though they embrace their own place on the continuum, recognize the opposite principle in themselves.

Cultural psychologists Markus and Conner gave a new prescription for psychological health:

> To build a more prosperous and peaceful world, everyone must be *both* independent and interdependent. This means that people who tend to be more independent will have to hone their interdependence, while people who tend to be more interdependent will need to polish their independence.[6]

From either side of *yin* or *yang*, though leanings or biases remain, one can begin to see the truth that Carl Jung spoke, "There is no such thing as a pure introvert or a pure extrovert. Such a person would be in the lunatic asylum."[7] As an impure introvert, you have drops of *yang* inside you. Being your complete self means owning all aspects of who you are and seeking to maintain your personal balance. Embrace your introverted uniqueness and your need for interdependence at the same time.

BALANCED LEADERSHIP

The case of King George III is not an isolated case. Long before George, and now long after, we still hold to a potentially outdated and outmoded idea of singular leadership. Most organizations have someone, a singular individual, at the top. The problems of the top are infamous. It's lonely up there, isolating. Most individuals were never made for the level of stress carried by the solo leader, and it tends to impact their health and well-being as well as their leadership effectiveness.

The answer is obvious. No one leader has all it takes to lead well. Each has something needed, but no single person has everything. To lead well, we need to lead plurally. *Plural leadership* provides the balance needed to make the best decisions on a consistent basis. Life was made to have this balance (*he*) between the *yin* and *yang* aspects of leadership. The differences between leaders should be valued, embraced and leveraged for the collective good of the team or organization. This is holistic team leadership, leadership that includes traits from all the four quadrants of DISC working together for optimal results.

THE FOUR QUADRANTS OF DISC

Using the DISC model helps us conceive not only of the differences between the two worlds of *yin* and *yang*, or of introversion and extroversion, but also to see the nuances between all four quadrants of the model. Putting both halves together, here are the four quadrants of DISC.

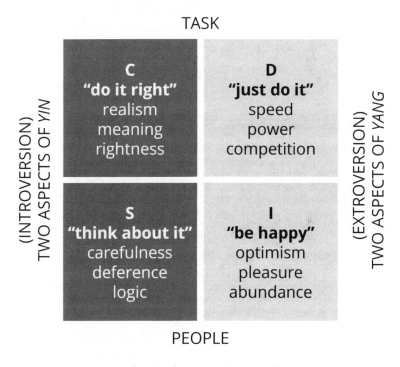

Figure 4. The four quadrants of DISC.

The DISC model is values-neutral, meaning that all places on the assessment are positive. There are no good or bad behavioral styles, only different. Because strengths occur in each of the four quadrants of DISC, traits that are needed on the leadership team as a whole occur in each. The whole team, drawing from the different strengths of D, I, S, and C, leads the organization into a holistic vision of the good life.

THE GOOD LIFE: WHOLENESS

Human civilization, according to many ancient traditions, began as one composite whole. Over time, we have degenerated into many warring factions and sects. We have become polarized as male against female, white against black, extrovert against introvert, *yang* against *yin*. This struggle is not new. According to the Jewish Scriptures, the third person on earth, Cain (*yang*), killed the fourth person, Abel (*yin*), as a result of the failure to value one another and the differences between them.[8] There is a general principle of decline in the world all around us. This may well include the tendency for these things needing balance to be divided from one another, leading to imbalance.[9] We are constantly breaking apart things that need to be held together.

The good life, then, will occur when these differences no longer serve as dividers but as reasons to cooperate with and celebrate one another. The good society would embrace the diversity built into the world all around us. All people would be valued for who they are in their uniqueness. None would be held down, mistreated or oppressed. All of our differences would be celebrated as beautiful expressions of the variety that makes life on this planet worth living.

That society would rightly balance the ideas of *hedonia* and *eudaimonia*, pleasure and meaning, in a composite concept called *wholeness*. It is this cultural revolution that many are working toward. Will we ever achieve this superior society? It remains to be seen. While we wait for cultural change, however, we can be about the business of creating our own personal revolution, our good life.

The good life for us as individuals is a life of congruence, authenticity and purpose connected to happiness, both personal and collective. Living and leading as our authentic self is the goal of the rest of this book. The goal of our personal revolution is a radical self-acceptance and affirmation of the goodness of who we are in all spheres of life, leaving no room for the debilitating effects of things in our past. This is the ideal toward which we move. Sadly, for many introverted leaders, life experiences to this point have not matched this vision. We have been acting out our part on the wrong stage, reading the wrong lines.

REFLECTION QUESTIONS

When I've had the privilege to work as part of a well-balanced leadership team, I've been my happiest and most fulfilled. Answer these questions as you reflect on the need for balance:

1. Do you agree that the singular leader (like King George III or even better than George) is problematic? Why or why not?

2. What do you think of the Continental Congress's solution to the need for balanced leadership?

3. Describe your need for balance between your *independent self* (the you that has unique strengths) and your *interdependent self* (the you that needs others). What happens to you if this balance is lost?

4. Do you believe introverted and extroverted leaders can work together in a complementary fashion? If so, how can they do it?

5. How would you define or describe the "good life"?

6. Have you ever felt like you were performing on the wrong stage? Describe how you knew it was the wrong venue and what you took away from those ill-fitting experiences.

PART TWO

Your Role So Far

"All the men and women merely players."

—William Shakespeare

Figuring out there were two stages and, at either extreme, two types of people, was the beginning of my personal revolution. Once these became real to me, I began to move through the other stages of cultural identity development. I experienced dissonance and confusion, wondering who I was and what it meant to be introverted in our society. I felt some healthy anger and sadness as I resisted the dominant stereotypes that I discovered were even inside of me. I thought deeply and introspectively about the nature of introversion, its strengths and challenges. I continue to move toward articulation and awareness, being able to experience my optimal identity as an introvert and a leader and to appreciate the extroverts who bring complementary traits. It's a work in progress.

Thus far, we've looked at the cultural context, the tank in which we swim and lead. Culture has tremendous power and is much bigger than any one of us. Understanding the nature of our cultural struggle is step one. *Grabbing hold of our own congruently introverted definition of the good life gives us a new vision for our future. Until now, we've all been acting on the extroverted stage of life with varying degrees of positive or negative responses to our performance.*

In part two, we'll look at who we are fundamentally and how we've been impacted so far. What I've learned from hundreds of introverted leaders in both formal and informal interviews is that each one's experience is different. We can't assume that all introverts have followed the same path and have experienced the same things. In this section, we're retracing our steps in the past. For some, the past has been relatively painless. For others, the opposite is true.

Part two needs to be contextualized to your story. If you've been through a lot, I hope it brings a degree of comfort, hope and meaning. If you've been through little, I hope it brings deeper empathy for others who have suffered more and prepares you for some potentially troubled spots ahead.

5

Fictions & Facts

"Ye shall know the truth and the truth shall make you mad."

—Aldous Huxley

John felt confused and discouraged after his supervisor told him he needed to be more outgoing. His coworkers in the sales department had told him similar things. He thought of himself as "outgoing" and wondered what they were seeing that suggested he wasn't. It was true he didn't particularly like parties or large networking events, but he really loved people in smaller doses, especially those he had formed deep relationships with. Some of his closest friends would offer the good-natured complaint that they couldn't "shut John up." Once he got going on a topic about which he was passionate, with someone who felt safe to him, John was highly social and communicative.

Sally had a similar problem. Her new boss told her she needed to contribute more in the weekly staff meetings. Most of the time, however, she felt unable to offer good thoughts in the middle of his famous brainstorming sessions. It frustrated her that her best ideas seemed to come first thing in the morning after "sleeping on it." In the moment, she felt like a deer frozen by the brightness of headlights. Her brain just seemed to spin out of control with thoughts during meetings, but she was rarely able to interrupt that neural process and get it to spit out a result.

Joe was struggling, too. The overall pace of the start-up business he had recently joined was killing him. Though he hadn't told anyone else at work how he felt, they could see the fairly obvious signs of stress. He wasn't sleeping well. He was becoming a bit short with people at work and home, and he had a hard time focusing on his bottom-line results. To make matters worse, one of his extroverted coworkers, Jeff, had suggested that he seemed depressed and might want to see someone about that. Jeff said his wife had been depressed, but once she got meds she was much easier to live with. "Lots of people are depressed; it's not that big a deal these days," Jeff said, in an attempt to cheer Joe up.

John, Sally and Joe's boss, Phil, who oversees all three of them, recently hired a professional coach to work with each of them. He believed in them and really wanted to see them improve their performance and be happier. The stated goals for each, given by Phil to the shared coach, were

- John—increase positivity, improve attitude, build larger network of relationships

- Sally—think better on her feet, provide more timely feedback during staff meetings

- Joe—pick up the pace, push harder for better results, reach higher performance goals, bring more energy to the team, cheer up

What's wrong with these coaching objectives for these individuals? Why might this coach be set up for failure? How could we adjust these coaching goals to better fit the individuals involved and to improve their health and the overall health of the organization?

John, Sally and Joe recently took several assessments in preparation for their work with the coach. One was the DISC. All three of them came out as high on the S and C dimensions, in other words, as more introverted. The goals given to the coach failed to reflect an understanding of introversion that is far too common in our *yang*-biased culture. In this chapter, we'll examine many commonly held cultural myths about introversion and the realities that underlie it. Had John, Sally and Joe's boss, Phil, understood these things, their respective situations might have been different.

Phil is at a crossroads. If he begins to better understand the introverted nature of his three employees and manage them accordingly, John, Sally and Joe will likely far exceed the results Phil would like to see. If he doesn't learn about the nature of introversion and continues to try to make all three of his employees more extroverted, he'll experience the opposite.

YANG FICTIONS (ABOUT INTROVERSION)

Phil is not alone. Most of us have many areas of confusion related to introversion in U.S. society. Cultural myths perpetuate the supremacy of the dominant cultural values, in this case, *yang*. In Western culture, introverts live under much misunderstanding and invalidation. Consider some common myths about introversion that our dominant culture, including introverts within it, often perpetuates:

Introversion is shyness. Just as the news reporter wrongly used the words "withdrawn" and "introverted" as synonyms to describe the behavior of the soldier who had moved away from his group, we often hear the word "shy" used as a synonym for introversion. The problem is that this completely misunderstands the nature of introversion and of shyness.

Shyness is about anxiety, social phobia, a lack of social skills and low self-esteem.[1] Introversion, as we'll see, is not. Introverts sometimes simply prefer to be alone or with a few close friends. Shyness, a struggle that afflicts forty to fifty percent of the U.S. population, is something that both introverts and extroverts can struggle with. Shy people are acutely self-conscious, which hinders them from the social relationships they seek. This experience is more painful for shy extroverts than for shy introverts. In any case, these two, often-confused aspects of personality, in reality, are not even correlated.

Introverts are antisocial. Yang culture continues to attempt to connect introversion with people like the "Unabomber" or the perpetrators of famous school massacres. Introverts are portrayed as withdrawn loners living away from the rest of society, curmudgeons. Introverts are not antisocial. Most of us love people, just in different doses and durations than extroverts. We normally want to have fewer deeper relationships. We normally aren't drawn to huge gatherings of people. Most of us don't like small talk very much. When we find ourselves in a larger gathering, we'll usually find one person and move to the edge of the crowd. The best way to describe this way of being is that we are "differently social."

Introversion is a choice. We'll deal more in depth with this myth in chapter six. For now, please note that introversion is no more of a choice than any other hereditary trait. At least fifty percent and likely more of our introverted traits are the result of heredity.[2] There seems to be a fairly uniform distribution of temperamental differences, including the introversion-extroversion trait, that are simply assigned to us at birth. This explains why my family was composed of an extroverted father, an introverted mother, an extroverted brother, an introverted brother, an ambiverted sister, and me. The cycle continues. I married an ambivert and, together, we have an ambiverted daughter, an extroverted daughter, and an introverted daughter. As their father,

I could clearly see my daughters' different temperaments from early childhood.

Introversion is curable. This is possibly the most irritating myth to face. *Yang* culture and its obsession with happiness and power are convinced there is something pathological about being introverted. Because it is often seen culturally as something to be cured, the psychological and psychiatric communities seek to include it as diagnostic criteria for various personality disorders and other mental health problems.[3] In the international psychological community, introversion is already diagnosable. In case you're interested, the World Health Organization (WHO) has created two diagnoses that might alarm you: *301.21—introverted personality; 313.22—introverted disorder of childhood.*[4]

Fortunately, the attempts to add introversion into diagnostic criteria here in the United States have thus far failed, though not for lack of effort.[5] While creating the most recent American diagnostic manual released in 2013, *Diagnostic and Statistical Manual of Mental Disorders, Fifth Edition* (DSM-V), proposals were submitted to the committee to have introversion included as a diagnostic component of several personality disorders, similar to the WHO criteria. This sounds like conspiracy theory or paranoia, but sadly it's not. There is a cultural agenda in the West that for some time now has sought to pathologize introversion and other related aspects of *yin* culture, things like sadness, fear, submissiveness, non-aggression.[6] If introversion is a normal and healthy way to be human, then obviously the attempts to pathologize it or to tell us we need to be cured of it are futile, yet still irksome and hurtful.

Introverts can't be leaders. This is the myth I encountered that evening at the conference banquet and have encountered many times and in many ways throughout my life. This is the heart of this book. This myth adds to the invalidation we feel as introverted people, often being seen as somehow deficient, another layer that claims we can't lead, either. Many of the stories you've read and will read are derived from real-life accounts of introverts who have been told they can't lead by people using the extrovert ideal as a bogus filter.

In addition to these five popular myths about introversion, there are many more Western cultural fictions and misunderstandings related to introversion. The nature of myths is that they are highly contagious and influence everyone, even those who suffer as a result of them. See how you do on the following:

1. The percentage of the U.S. population that is introverted is:

    a. 25%   b. 33%   c. 40%   d. 50%   e. 66%

2. The percentage of CEOs in the United States that are introverted versus extroverted is:

    a. 10%   b. 20%   c. 30%   d. 40%   e. 50%

3. With highly motivated proactive workers, the best leaders are:

    a. introverts   b. extroverts   c. ambiverts

    d. neither   e. doesn't matter

4. With passive workers needing external motivation, the best leaders are:

    a. introverts   b. extroverts   c. ambiverts

    d. neither   e. doesn't matter

5. According to leadership experts Peter Drucker and Jim Collins, good leaders are typically highly charismatic individuals:

    a. true   b. false

6. Introversion is a protected class in terms of hiring and firing (like race, gender, religion, etc.):

a. true   b. false

7. In general, what kinds of people tend to perform best in sales:

a. introverts   b. ambiverts   c. extroverts

d. doesn't matter

8. The percentage of gifted children who are introverted is:

a. 20%   b. 40%   c. 60%   d. 80%   e. 100%

9. Which of these creative geniuses is extroverted?

a. Ben Franklin   b. Walt Disney   c. Albert Einstein

d. Mark Zuckerberg   e. Charles Darwin

10. Which of these high performers is not an introvert?

a. Steve Martin   b. Oprah Winfrey   c. Donald Trump

d. Michael Jordan   e. Christina Aguilera[7]

INTROVERTED FACTS

The true nature of introversion is widely misunderstood in our culture. Three main areas of truth regarding introversion are helpful for all of us, introverts and extroverts alike, to increase our understanding. Knowledge is power. Introversion, contrary to popular myth, is about physiology, energy and orientation.

Introversion is physiological. How many of us have been told, "It's all in your head," as it pertains to our introversion. People who don't understand what introversion is coach us to "get over it." Since technology can show us the formerly mysterious inner workings of the human brain, it's now clear that differences between extroverts and introverts are not imagined but very real as determined by our biology.

At its core, introversion is about sensitivity to outside stimulation. The key to understanding introversion begins at the base of the brain through something called the ascending reticular activating system (ARAS). We all have one. This is the place where the spinal cord connects to the brain, where outside stimulation enters the brain after being retrieved from the senses. From that point on, the differences between extroverts and introverts are visible now that we have functional MRIs, positron emission topographical (PET) scans and similar technologies. The physiology couldn't be more different. Ironically, "it's all in your head" appears to be quite accurate when taken more literally.

Where extroverts and introverts differ is in the optimal level of arousal.[8] There is an optimal level of arousal for human beings where we are neither under-stimulated (falling asleep) nor over-stimulated (stressed out). Think of that level as the horizontal line in figure 5, at the midpoint between high and low arousal.

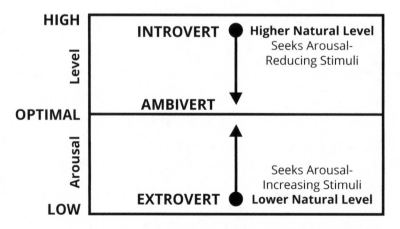

Figure 5. Differing levels of arousal.

Introverts and extroverts have different set points relative to that optimal level. Introverts run naturally at a much higher base level of arousal. As illustrated, they have to bring themselves down to the optimal level. Extroverts are the opposite. They run at a much lower base level of arousal and need to be pushed up to the optimal level to feel good. This is why the extrovert seeks outwardly stimulating experiences to feel better, closer to the optimal level, while the introvert avoids similar overly stimulating environments and prefers calmer, quieter experiences that allow them to come down to the optimal level. Obviously, ambiverts fall somewhere in between, more naturally near the optimal level. If this theory is correct, and there is good evidence to suggest it is, sensitivity to stimulation is the leading trait of introversion-extroversion.

In addition to differences in terms of arousal set points, introverts' and extroverts' brains also follow different *neural pathways* in response to outside stimuli. Dr. Marti Olsen Laney, the leading expert in understanding these differences, has helped to explain the importance of this biological reality, taking very complicated data from brain scans and simplifying it to assist our understanding.[9]

For extroverts, the path moves quickly through five areas: from the base of the brain where the spinal cord connects, through the hypothalamus, the thalamus, and the amygdala (where emotions connect with actions), straight to the temporal and motor areas of the brain. The introverted path is much longer and different (see figure 6). An introvert has a more circuitous path: the stimulus enters at the base of the brain as well, but follows a different path through the hypothalamus, the other side of the thalamus, through Broca's area (where inner dialogue happens), the frontal lobe (where thinking and reasoning happens), and then finally to the hippocampus and the amygdala (where thoughts and feelings connect).

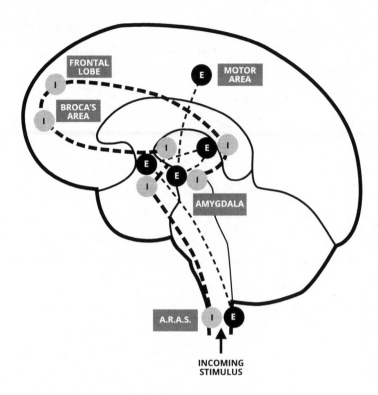

Figure 6. Differing neural pathways

This reality begins to help you understand why Sally sometimes has a deer in the headlights look in her boss's famous brainstorming sessions. Her brain is pushing thoughts down a longer path through Broca's area and her frontal lobe and processing data in an entirely different manner and place in her brain than the extroverts sitting at the same table. Though some of her extroverted coworkers perceive her as having no thoughts on the subject, in reality, she has too much going on upstairs. If we wired her brain to show activity during the brainstorming, these different areas toward the front of her head would light up.

Not only are there different neural pathways for introverts and extroverts, each also uses different neurotransmitters, brain chemicals, to process information. Introverts run primarily on the *acetylcholine* transmitter, which gives them a good feeling when thinking or feeling deeply. They have higher natural levels of *dopamine*, the chemical related to rewards that is released in conjunction with adrenaline in stimulating experiences, and are much more sensitive to surges of additional dopamine.

Too much dopamine can actually feel painful, which is why many introverts avoid overstimulation. The activity and noise in a large room full of too many people has a real physiological trigger for introverts. Extroverts are different. They are naturally dopamine deficient and crave the release of adrenaline and dopamine, the rush that comes from excitement. They feel best when surrounded by lots of external stimulation. The same room that feels overwhelming to an introvert gives energy to an extrovert.

Lastly, extroverts and introverts rely on different halves of the autonomic nervous system. The autonomic (self-governing) nervous system controls all of those functions that we do without thinking (e.g., breathing, digesting, circulating, etc.). It is divided into two halves that ideally should work in good balance (*he*) with each other. The parasympathetic system relies on acetylcholine and has to do with "throttling down" and restoring the body after action.[10] The sympathetic nervous system works in the opposite direction. It uses dopamine and has to do with "throttling up" and preparing for action.

These two halves of the autonomic system each have important functions. Balance in this regard is often lacking on either end of the temperamental spectrum. Extroverts tend to favor the sympathetic side while introverts favor the parasympathetic. This may be a good argument for a slight advantage of ambiversion as a well-adjusted and well-balanced point between these two systems. In summary, extroverts' and introverts' brains and nervous systems function quite differently. The differences are not imaginary but actual physiological variances.

Introversion is about energy, where we get it, how we use it and how we renew it. Introverts tend to generate energy from within, needing far less external stimulation. They also tend to use it up more readily, requiring more frequent renewal. You may have noticed that extroverts and introverts tend to recharge differently. It's as if we have two different kinds of batteries. For the extrovert who has a lower set point, the outside stimulation is a recharging and renewing experience. For the introvert who has a higher set point, the absence of outward stimulation and instead calming peaceful experiences or even very active inward experiences are recharging and renewing. Many introverts renew in the process of turning inward toward deep thinking and contemplation. They may seek out a good book as a means of restoring energy.

This does not mean, however, that the only way for an introvert to be refreshed is in isolation. For many introverts, books are like friends. Sometimes reading or spending time alone thinking or resting can be a renewing experience. Other introverts are more social. For them, spending quality time with a good friend and experiencing the good feelings that come with genuine relationships and deep thinking together can similarly recharge their batteries.

Introversion is lastly a more *inward orientation*, inclined toward the world of abstract thoughts and concepts. While driving with my wife, she would often ask me, "Are you OK?" Apparently, my fully engaged brain was very active inwardly as I focused on my inner dialogue, driving the car on autopilot. As I learned more about introversion, I began to understand and explain to her that it's often loud and very active inside my head. The wheels are spinning as ideas or problems are being processed inwardly. I may not be saying anything, but it's not quiet inside. She and I have both learned that the constant internal dialogue seems to be the default setting and if she needs my full attention, I need to flip a switch. Extroversion is often the opposite, with less internal noise, responding more to external stimuli. Extroverts tend to be more naturally in the moment and less distracted by inner dialogue.

This inward orientation is a tremendous strength to be leveraged for introverts. Many complex problems require deep thinking and analysis that requires sustained focus. Issues that involve abstract concepts and principles are the natural domain of introverts. As long as we manage this strength and listen to our significant others when they need us to, this inward focus is a beautifully rich place of ideas and concepts that we were made to live in.

Introversion has nothing to do with shyness or being antisocial, is not pathological needing to be cured, and in no way disqualifies from leadership. It is a healthy physiological difference that runs on a different set point toward stimulation, has differing neural pathways and neurotransmitters, and has distinct energy management needs, along with a rich inner life. It has absolutely nothing to do with the stereotypes about introverts that dominate our cultural landscape. Fiction needs to be separated from fact. This is the first step in moving forward to be the leaders we were made to be.

REFLECTION QUESTIONS

Learning the ways I'm different physiologically and biologically has been a huge step forward. Understanding the science of introversion has dispelled many myths I was previously told or believed. Considering the facts you just learned about introverts, reflect on the following questions.

1. How does more accurate scientific knowledge help you better understand yourself?

2. What happens when you try to be more extroverted? Should you do it?

3. What surprised you in this chapter? What facts challenged your previous perception of introversion?

4. If introversion has a higher normal level of arousal, what happens when you are over-aroused? Describe your experience.

5. Are there any adrenaline-producing experiences that you like to have?

6. How do you recharge your batteries? What is the best thing for you to do when you feel depleted?

7. How loud is it in your head? What does it sound like inside? What kinds of things do you tend to focus on?

6

Nature & Nurture

"Whatever doesn't kill you makes you stronger."

—Friedrich Nietzsche, popularized by Kelly Clarkson

Life may be a stage, but acting is exhausting work for most of us. Each of us grows up in a different environment. We arrive in the world with a pre-wired disposition, but learn how to act in the context of a growing social reality. Meet three introverts who had very different experiences in their families of origin. Each of them learned about themselves and their temperaments from significant people in their lives. As it is for them, it is for each of us.

Ben had shown signs of introversion from birth. His parents noticed that he was, even as an infant, more prone to overstimulation. He was the youngest of three children in his family and the only boy. His two older sisters differed from each other. The oldest took after Mom, and the girl's extroverted and outgoing nature was praised. Ben's middle sister was like him in many ways, though actually far less social. Their mother, a socialite in their uppity community, "encouraged" her son to be more outgoing, to emerge from his room and join the parties that were frequently going on in their suburban home. Ben wondered if his desire to be alone was problematic, whether there was something wrong with him. Ben experienced a subtle form of rejection from his mother, even though she loved him.

Maryanna, like Ben, was a quieter, less boisterous child than her four siblings. She grew up on a dairy farm in rural Iowa and has fond memories every time she smells a cornfield after it rains. While many complain of their parochial school experience, Maryanna cherished her schooling as a wonderful time in her life. "The nuns were great," she remembered. She had none of the experiences popularized in the movies. The sisters by whom she was taught encouraged her to be who she was, to accept the way God had created her. Those formative experiences in Catholic school served her well. She grew into a very secure and confident young lady as a result. Maryanna's experience of acceptance by the nuns and her family of origin set her up to become who she is today.

Shaping experiences happen to us throughout life. Tim's early childhood was happy and he felt accepted in his mostly introverted family. It felt good to fit in. Throughout his adult life, he had experienced mostly positive experiences at work and school and felt secure in his abilities as a computer programmer working for a technology company. However, recent events had him second-guessing himself quite severely. An evaluation two months earlier with his new supervisor, Melanie, seemed to be the catalyst for his confusion. Up until that evaluation, he had always received positive, glowing feedback. Job reviews were actually something he looked forward to. This time it was different.

Melanie's "drive-bys" were infamous. Though no one would admit to noticing them, everyone could see them happening. She was the gregarious and driven vice president of Tim's manufacturing company. Everything was OK, or seemed to be, until she showed up. From the get-go, she always made Tim feel that he "didn't measure up" and that he "wasn't leadership material." He didn't just feel that way; she came right out and said it. These thoughts and feelings of self-doubt were new to him. When he told his story months later, there was still notable emotion in his voice as he spoke.

All of our lives, we are exposed to relationships with people who have either a nurturing and enhancing or detrimental effect on our personal and professional development and growth. Who we become is a result of several significant factors, beginning with the starting point, our inherited nature.

NATURE

I'm the proud owner of a golden retriever named Katy. One of the things I like most about Katy is her introversion. Have you noticed that certain breeds of dogs have certain predictable dispositions or temperaments? Katy is peaceful, loving, loyal and interdependent, all introverted traits. She's deathly afraid of thunder and we have a routine that we go through to comfort her every time we see clouds approaching and the possibility of lightning and the "t" word.

If breeds of dogs have certain inborn traits, do breeds or variations of humans similarly come into the world with a certain amount of hardwiring, a certain disposition? As explained in the last chapter, you as an introvert have a different arousal set point than the extroverts around you. Your brain takes different pathways and runs on different chemicals. You don't have to try to not like overstimulating experiences; it comes quite naturally and instinctively.

Experts seem to be slowly converging toward the truth that the nature versus nurture debate is not an either-or answer but both nature and nurture working together. On the nature side, it seems to be the case that we all come into the world with an innate disposition that places us at a particular location on the introvert-extrovert continuum. Most of us have a dominant leaning toward one side or the other just as most of us have a dominant hand. In many respects, we come with a preloaded operating system.[1]

Katy isn't just a dog (*canis*), she's a Golden Retriever. You're not just a human (*homosapien*), you're an (introverted/ambiverted/extroverted) human. It's interesting that we can be so clear about the importance of different subspecies in the animal kingdom and talk as if humanity is less complex. Katy, the golden retriever, is introverted, looking for love. Kevin, the betta fish we met earlier, is extroverted, looking for a fight. If the type of fish we are is our nature, the water we swim in is our tank. This is the other half of the equation, *nurture*.

NURTURE

Is that the answer, then? Are we simply a product of genetics? How does the nurture side of the debate figure in?

We are who we are according to our disposition *and* we exist in an environment, a culture and subcultures. It is important to understand that as much as the brain comes genetically predisposed in certain ways, it is also plastic, formed over time in response to stimuli, and develops in response to the environment.[2] As the renowned neuroscientist Daniel Siegel put it:

> Genes determine much of how neurons link up with each other, but equally important is that experience activates genes to influence this linkage process. . . . In fact, experience shapes brain structure. Experience is biology. How we treat our children changes who they are and how they will develop. Their brains need our parental involvement. Nature needs nurture.[3]

Nurture-abuse is a spectrum just like introversion-extroversion. It ranges on one extreme from nurture to the other extreme of abuse, with neglect or indifference in the middle. Ron Rohner is a psychologist and researcher who has dedicated his life to this area of nurture.[4] For over fifty years, he has been seeking to understand the impact of interpersonal rejection or acceptance, an environmental factor, on overall well-being. He began by focusing on parental relationships but has expanded his theory to include parental, romantic and other significant relationships throughout the life span.

Key to interpersonal acceptance-rejection theory (IPARTheory) is an understanding of the spectrum of responses from key attachment figures, such as parents. The model ranges from warmth (acceptance) through neglect to more overt rejection. Overt rejection would include all forms of abuse or mistreatment, including physical, emotional, verbal or sexual abuse, all communicating to the individual that they are not valued. Neglect, "undifferentiated rejection," as Rohner called it, is harder to see but has similarly adverse effects to more overt forms of abuse. In this way, no significant relationships are neutral. They are all either nurturing, neglectful or harmful. And they all affect us.

So, it's a combination of nature and nurture that shapes us into the person we become.[5] The environment can shape us positively or negatively. Without intending to, Ben's mother negatively shaped Ben's self-confidence. The nuns positively shaped the person Maryanna was becoming. Can you think of significant life experiences or relationships that have positively contributed to who you have become? Was there someone in your life that seemed to be there at a critical point in your personal journey?

That's how it was for Tim from the introduction to this chapter. Having just received the confusing feedback from Melanie in his first performance review with her, he was deeply troubled and confused. Fortunately, he was vaguely aware of another leader in the organization he suspected was also more introverted. He took the initiative and made an appointment with Miles to look for some clarity and direction.

Miles, coincidentally, had just finished *Quiet*, Susan Cain's book on the power of introversion, and was able not only to recommend the book to Tim but also to validate what Tim was feeling. Miles went on to explain how he was able to lead, quite successfully, in the organization as himself and stay true to his introverted nature. When asked about it years later, Miles hardly remembered the interaction he had had with Tim. For Tim, however, that brief exchange had been a lifesaver. Tim was validated and shown that who he was as an introverted leader was not something he needed to, nor could, change. Had Tim lacked that support from Miles, there is a good possibility his world may have continued to unravel. At critical points of our development, we each need someone like Miles, a coach and encourager, to help us on our way.

NURTURE IN AN EXPANDING WORLD

Most of us follow similar paths as our world expands over time. Our world is initially quite small, comprised of only ourselves and our immediate families. Over time, our world increases as the circle widens. At each of these wider circles, we have another opportunity to experience either positive or adverse relationships and their impact. Nurture actually begins in the womb. From the moment of conception, we are impacted by our mothers. Their stress levels, habits and even physical health have a direct impact on our prenatal development. Regardless of our situation in the womb, we are born and enter the world.

Most of us at birth began in a *family setting*. They were all different in terms of how many parents we had, how many siblings, the general health of the family system, and so on. Mine was an intact family with two parents, an extroverted father and introverted mother, and three siblings, a very extroverted oldest brother, an introverted brother, and an ambiverted sister. Others have had alternate "families" ranging from foster homes to orphanages. Whether we grew up in a traditional family or had alternate kinds of families, our initial environment was the first place that told us who we were.

My family of origin favored extroversion as the model of healthy human development. Being confident in oneself and asserting oneself were encouraged. I was different from the start. From ages three to four, my parents were a bit concerned about me and my development. My mother wrote (emphasis is my own):

His relationship with other children varies with their age. When he started preschool, he was *cordial* to the children, *almost shy.* . . . He is *afraid* to go to sleep without a night light. He *imagines* shapes at the window, etc., since seeing *The Wizard of Oz* and the witch with the green face several months ago. . . . He seems to have a *very keen mind.* He *learns quickly* and *retains well* what he has learned. . . . He has a *good vocabulary* and *forms long sentences* and has *very good diction.* He *talks all the time* [in the family] and we try to give him our full attention and really listen. . . . [He] held a stick horse for a long time and *watched* another little girl ride hers—but he *couldn't get up enough courage* to get on his. . . . During song time, *just watched* today. Part of the time *turned around to see what was going on behind him.* . . . [He] went to puzzle table first, *as he has every week* [routine]. As he works, he *watches every other child* at the table and *looks at children around the room to see what is going on.* . . . [He] went up to the front to show his leopard hat and mask, but *would not talk to the teacher.* This was his first time in front of the group. . . . [He] sang the songs he knew well, but *if he was not sure of the words he would not try to sing at all.* The teacher asked him where he'd like to go on the train and he *smiled but did not answer. I don't know if he could think of a place* [difficult to think in the moment]. . . . *Very attentive* during song time. *Watched closely but didn't join in.* Was *very quiet* during rest time, *very alert to everything happening* [higher level of sensitivity]. . . . At school, in September, he was an *observer*—he would not sing or use his hands, he would not participate in the bells at all. Now *he usually does unless he is tired or not feeling well* [energy level]. [After watching The Wizard of Oz again] has since seen the Wicked Witch of the West lurking around our home. He doesn't like to go in certain parts of the house alone [fear, vivid imagination]. I don't ever recall the other children having something like this last so long and intensely. . . . He climbed to the top of the parallel bars and *could not get enough courage* to swing out so he *climbed back down the ladder* [no risk-taking gene]. [6]

Too passive. Too timid. Too quiet. Too pensive. Hyper-alert to the environment. Holding back too much. Not being assertive enough. Having more emotional reactivity than the other siblings. Being too afraid. For introverts in an extroverted world, looking back on our experiences, this may be the first time we ran into a vague sense of not fitting in. Before we had words to explain the feeling, it was stored as a more raw emotional experience in our amygdala, the part of our brain triggered in emotional experiences.

Your interaction with family is the first of a series of widening circles you encounter throughout your life that help shape how you see yourself. Figure 7 depicts our ever-expanding circles of group participation. For introverts, this means that most of these groups will share the cultural bias toward extroversion and against introversion.

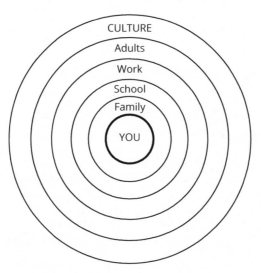

Figure 7. Widening circles of our world.

From your family circle, you ventured out into the second circle of your world, *school*. Even if you were homeschooled, you likely had group activities that involved other children where you encountered new people and continued to form a sense of who you were.

Though many introverts are "gifted," school can be a difficult place for them. Jill Burruss and Lisa Kaenzig have studied the impact of the school environment on gifted introverts and summarized their findings as follows:

> School is not a positive experience for many gifted introverts. It can be loud, crowded, superficial, boring, overstimulating, and focused on action, not reflection. . . . Many teachers report being extroverts. It is very difficult for an extrovert to understand an introvert. Therefore, the teacher may see the introverted student as someone with a problem, not as simply someone with a different personality type.[7]

Teachers push for more vocal participation in class discussions, can be obsessed with students working in groups, and often work in ways that don't support the quieter students in the room. For the most part, I was fortunate and had very nurturing teachers in elementary school. Almost all of them stand out to me as loving, accepting and encouraging adults in my life who believed in me and in my abilities. Though many of the teachers in junior high and high school were also nurturing, those years proved to be a bit more difficult due mainly to my extrovert-biased peers.

One of those extroverted peers was my friend Jerry. Having switched from private to public schools in seventh grade, I was new to the junior high school I attended. Jerry was in just about all of my classes that first year, as well as the following six of my secondary schooling. Because he was extroverted, taller and more outgoing, I likely connected with him to help me connect with the others in my classes. Our friendship throughout junior high and high school was based on me accepting that I was "less than" Jerry. He made sure I knew my status on almost a daily basis. I was glad to go off to college and have a fresh start.

After school, your third widening of the circle occurred when you began to *work*. Maybe you worked during school and these circles overlapped in time. In that work environment, you met even more people: coworkers, supervisors, subordinates, clients or customers, vendors, and more. All of these relationships began to give you feedback, covertly or overtly, about who you are and how you fit in.

For me, my first career after college was in architecture, an introvert-friendly profession. Many architects are introverts, enjoying hours working alone on the details of architectural projects. Introverts are often highly creative, which connects well to design professions. Other introvert-friendly fields include corporate law (as opposed to trial law), accounting, technology, engineering, academia, psychotherapy, the military and certain religious occupations within more contemplative-oriented groups. Difficult work environments for introverts often include sales organizations, marketing, and certain religious occupations within more extrovert-oriented groups.

Most of us will work for forty-five to fifty years, all the while gaining feedback, both overtly and covertly, about who we are and how we fit in. Our career path will be populated by different kinds of people and different experiences that will have either a positive or negative effect on our leadership development and sense of self.

We also experience significantly shaping *adult relationships* outside of the workplace, represented by the fourth circle. Many of us form romantic attachments and find partners to share our lives with. All of us form social friendships and working relationships at different levels and in different places in our adult lives. All of these relationships give us even more information about who we are and how we fit, confirming or disconfirming existing self-perceptions.

I met my wife in high school at the church I attended. She was more extroverted. Our phone calls in those days were probably ninety percent her words with my occasional "yeahs" or "uh-huhs." Our married life together has been a great example of the need for a balance between *yin* and *yang*. She's helped me understand that who I am, as an introvert, is OK. She has been a great counter to many of the negative experiences I've had in life connected to being introverted.

THE EFFECT OF RELATIONSHIPS

What is the net effect of these life experiences in a widening circle? We still cite the child's rhyme about sticks and stones. It is quite popular to quote the adage, "Whatever doesn't kill you makes you stronger." Kelly Clarkson took that phrase and pushed it to the top of the charts in our extroverted culture. Nietzsche and Clarkson, however, are wrong; whatever doesn't kill you probably makes you weaker. In a recent *Psychology Today* article, Noam Shpancer disagreed with Nietzsche.[8] Shpancer used the examples of traumatized children, children who have grown up in tough neighborhoods, and even 9/11 survivors to prove his case. Adversity doesn't automatically, necessarily or even eventually make us stronger. Instead, there are long-term effects from such adverse life experiences.[9]

Life experiences matter. They can have a shaping influence on who we become but not in a deterministic way. It would actually be better not to go through deeply traumatic experiences and to have a lesser history of hardship. But, we cannot go back and undo the past. Hardship may make us weaker, but it doesn't have to take us down. We may walk with a metaphorical limp. But we can walk nonetheless. The different relationships we have with others are powerful, but the net effect on us is mediated through one additional variable, our interpretation of these life events.

How you interpret life events is related to your operating system, your temperament. Optimism directly connects to extroversion, just as clearly as pessimism connects naturally to introversion. The same input, by the time it gets interpreted and processed, does not yield the same output. This explains, in part, why similar life experiences take a larger or smaller toll on different people. Having support through negative experiences can help minimize the impact.

The real equation is nature plus nurture (good or bad) plus our interpretation of our experiences equals the net effect. Figure 8 illustrates the conceptual equation.

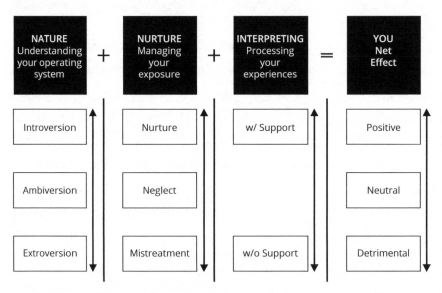

Figure 8. The net effect of nature + nurture + interpretation.

Each aspect of our experience in the equation has the potential to result in a positive or detrimental net effect on us. There is a range of possibilities (indicated by the arrows) at each point in the process. These all combine together, creating a cumulative effect.

Every human being comes preloaded with a natural disposition. To that we add the effect of our nurture or lack thereof but only as it is interpreted with or without the support of others. Often the natural pessimism of an introvert or the natural optimism of an extrovert will largely flavor their interpretation of life events. The net effect is the result of those life experiences interpreted, mediated or mitigated by those around us. Having supportive people to help us through adversity can make a big difference in the net effect of a bad thing, especially for introverts.

For Tim, it was the supportive relationship with Miles that gave him the space to reevaluate Melanie's comments. Miles played a vital role in helping Tim reframe the experience in a way that neutralized at least some of the power of Melanie's stereotype. Without that support, where would Tim have been? He could have toughed it out on his own, but as someone who understands healthy interdependence, he benefitted from the power of the connection with Miles to get through the adversity together.

Whatever doesn't kill us doesn't make us stronger. Nurture or the lack of it, being with or without adequate social support, is a critical factor in human development. Life experiences can have lasting and permanent impacts on people. How we treat one another matters. There's another more tangible element in our environment. The places and spaces in which we work and live also have an impact on our well being and productivity as introverts.

THE EFFECT OF THE BUILT ENVIRONMENT

We most often think of nurture as an interpersonal thing, and that is mostly correct. Nurture, primarily, is about treating others as worthwhile and investing time and effort to help them become who they were meant to be. There is, however, one additional aspect of nurture that we need to consider before we leave this subject, our *physical environment*.[10] As an architect, I am convinced that physical environment also impacts performance and overall sense of well-being in the workplace. I have always believed that better spaces contribute to better living and better work. Physical environment matters.

We have been using a fishbowl and water (or even the fake plants) metaphorically to describe culture and the interpersonal environment that surround us. We can also think of this analogy more literally. What are the most important issues for an introvert's work space? There has been a lot of press lately on what an utter failure open-office floor plans are.[11] This is especially true for introverts.

A colleague of mine was recently coaching an introverted client. This client, we'll call him Juan, was actually doing his work in a common area in the building because his cubicle was so loud and had so many distractions that he simply couldn't get anything done there. What do you suppose the impact was on Juan's performance trying to get his work done in a common area? What might the positive impact be of Juan's superiors providing him a private office, with a door, where he can focus on his work? Some of the things in the office environment to consider for introverts include

- Do I have a door I can shut to have quiet and focus? Should I post office hours to prevent walk-ins? If I don't have a door, what can I do to maintain quiet and focus?

- Do I have adequate privacy? Can I talk privately on the phone with others? Can I have private face-to-face conversations? Is there a conference room I can use?

- If I'm in a cubicle, how can I create a sense of privacy or quiet? Can I use headphones? Other means?

- How much traffic, noise or distraction is near my workplace? How can I reduce this?

- Do I have the ability to create different lighting in my work space? Can I turn off the fluorescent bulbs and plug in ambient task lighting?

- Is there flexibility to work alternate office hours so I can have some time early in the morning or later in the evening that is freer from distractions or interruptions?

We begin with our nature, an introverted disposition or temperament. We add environmental influences, life experiences and interpersonal relationships, both good and bad, in our ever-expanding world. Those influences are interpreted with or without the support of others and by our own ability to choose our reality. Lastly, this is most often happening inside a built environment, a work or home space. The net effect of all these can be found in who you are now and who you are becoming.

REFLECTION QUESTIONS

My temperament has been the one constant over my lifespan. As an introvert, I've experienced both nurturing and detrimental relationships. How about you?

1. What is your operating system, your nature? What is true about you at the core, your automatic responses to certain kinds of stimuli? Why is it important to understand your nature?

2. What kinds of nurturing experiences have you had to date? Which has been the strongest influence on who you have become, how you see yourself?

3. What have been the most adverse experiences you have had to date? How have those shaped who you have become? How does your interpretation of those events affect this process?

4. Are you comfortable in your skin (understand and like your operating system)?

5. Describe the nurture, neglect or mistreatment you have experienced in your expanding world. How have these experiences shaped who you've become?

   a. Your family of origin or alternative family?

   b. Your school experiences? Teachers? Professors? Students?

   c. Your work experiences? Bosses? Coworkers?

   d. Your adult relationships? Spouses or significant others? Friends?

6. How does your "office" environment work for you? Do you have adequate privacy? Can you focus on your work without unnecessary distractions?

7

Being In & Being Out

"Man is a social animal. He who lives without society is either a beast or God."

—Aristotle

"It is not good for man to be alone."

—God

"No man is an island."

—John Donne

Becky was struggling. Since her promotion from one department to another in her company, she was experiencing quite a bit of emotional pain and cognitive disruption. Life felt less meaningful than it had in previous years. She wanted to be happy about the new opportunity to lead, but though she would never tell anyone else, she knew that it just wasn't happening for her, at least not yet.

Why was she feeling this way? The interoffice politics at Becky's firm were similar to the dynamics in many organizations. In her company, people were almost always promoted from within. This was mostly a good thing; it gave hope for advancement to those already in the organization. But it also had a downside. When someone was promoted within, it almost always meant that others who applied from inside were not chosen. Those in the new department who had been passed over for the position were either knowingly or unknowingly making Becky feel unwanted in the group.

Just how serious is this problem of exclusion or ostracism? How much damage can a little cold shoulder do to someone? In Becky's case, quite a bit. It is a big deal to be accepted by the group.

Becky is an introvert. This means, among other things, that she tends to see life more interdependently through the lens of *yin*. She is also more sensitive to the perceived rejection of the group by that same principle. In her new role, she was having a difficult time trying to lead those whom she does not feel a part of.

TO NEED TO BELONG

If the stereotype about introverts like Becky were true, that she doesn't really like people anyway and prefers to be a loner, she wouldn't feel the pain of not belonging in relation to her team at work. As you know, that stereotype is completely false. All of us, extroverts, introverts or ambiverts, have a fundamental need to belong according to social psychologists Roy Baumeister and Mark Leary.[1] In their review of literature throughout the last three decades of the twentieth century, they identified a persistently validated principle: *we need to belong*. This need to belong is universal across all times and cultures and includes our need to have frequent personal connections in stable, continuing, emotionally vital relationships. A lack of this type of connectedness with others is shown to be detrimental to all aspects of human well-being and development. So, Moses, quoting God, and others were right, "It's not good to be alone."

This need to belong can be shown to be perhaps the most basic and fundamental need we have as human beings. Abraham Maslow, likely an introvert, postulated that human needs could be understood hierarchically. Beginning with basic survival needs, Maslow thought we build toward higher levels of need fulfillment culminating in our self-actualization, fulfilling the purpose for which we exist.

His original study of seven contemporaries and nine historical figures who he considered to be self-actualized included a disproportionate percentage of introverts.[2] Further, his list of qualities in self-actualized people shown in table 1 leans heavily toward the *yin* side of the equation. Here's his list of self-actualized traits:

• Clear perception of reality	• Humility & respect for others
• Acceptance (self & reality)	• Ethical
• Spontaneity	• Sense of humor (self-effacing)
• Problem-centered (outside of self)	• Creativity
• Solitude-seeking	• Resistant to enculturation
• Autonomous	• Imperfect (all emotions of normal people)
• Having peak (transcendent) experiences	• Values
• Desire to help all people	

Table 1. Maslow's characteristics of self-actualized people

Not surprisingly, you'll notice that many of the traits connect to more introverted people. This confirms the reality of bias in all of us, including Maslow.

Over time, his original five-level hierarchy was extended to his final version of eight levels shown in figure 9.

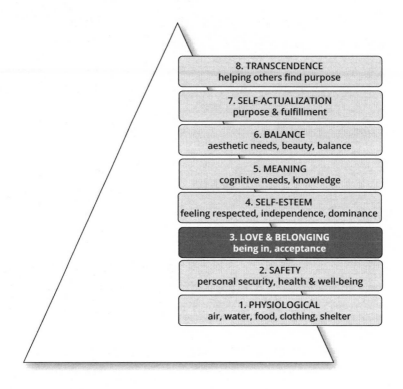

Figure 9. Maslow's expanded hierarchy of needs.

Interestingly, Maslow put love and belonging as a level-three need. Love and belonging as a need, however, can exist in places devoid of safety or physiological needs being met. In that sense, love and belonging, as Baumeister and Leary argued, is just as basic a human need as Maslow's bottom two. Social scientist Pamela Rutledge agreed. She recently commented in response to Maslow's theory,

> Needs are not hierarchical. Life is messier than that. Needs are, like most other things in nature, an interactive, dynamic system, but they are anchored in our ability to make social connections. Maslow's model needs rewiring so it matches our brains. Belongingness is the driving force of human behavior, not a third-

tier activity. The system of human needs from bottom to top, shelter, safety, sex, leadership, community, competence and trust, are dependent on our ability to connect with others. Belonging to a community provides the sense of security and agency that makes our brains happy and helps keep us safe.[3]

She brilliantly reconfigured Maslow's model as shown in figure 10:

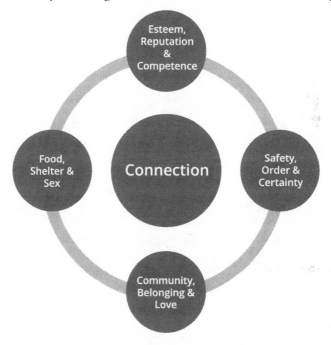

Figure 10. Rutledge's model of needs.[4]

Being connected to others in a meaningful way is central to our well-being. We are social creatures and are not made to do life alone. Rutledge's model beautifully reorganizes the needs Maslow discussed by recognizing this core human reality.

C. S. Lewis, known most for his children's books and Christian theology, was also an astute observer of human behavior. As an unofficial social psychologist in his day, he brilliantly described one of the most powerful forces in the human race. The "inner ring," as Lewis called it, is an unofficial group that is never spoken of and yet known by all. People are either in ("us") or out ("them"). It has existed for each of us from the time we began forming relationships. It can be found in preschools, high schools, offices, religious communities and even families. As Lewis pointed out:

> In all men's lives at certain periods, and in many men's lives at all periods between infancy and extreme old age, one of the most dominant elements is the desire to be inside the local Ring, and the terror of being left outside.[5]

Not belonging. Being left outside the circle. The terror. It is this sense of being outside the in-group that evokes such powerful emotions in humans. Our fear of being out is so strong that when we find ourselves outside of the circle, our sense of meaning in the world is directly affected. Research has shown a direct correlation between levels of belonging and meaningfulness (Maslow's level-five need).

In fact, it has been shown that "social exclusion could threaten people at such a basic level that it would impair their sense of meaningful existence."[6] Experiencing social exclusion or ostracism reduces our sense of meaning in all four areas—family, school, work, and adult relationships. This is precisely what was impacting Becky so strongly. Our need to belong also intersects with another individual trait, our gender.

BELONGING AND GENDER

I currently live in Idaho, where men are "men." They hunt, fish, ride motorcycles and do other "manly things." I read books, write, play tennis and am great at working with others from a place of deep empathy. I've never hunted or killed an animal in my entire life. Because of this reality, I often feel disconnected from some of the male discussions around me. A similar challenge exists for women who are more aggressive, driven or direct. In fact, our culture has a word for women like that, which I refuse to use. (Did I mention I have three daughters?) What does it take to be "one of the guys" or "one of the girls"? Oftentimes, belonging is connected to gender.

Think back to what you learned about *yin* and *yang*. *Yin* corresponds more to female gender stereotypes like receptivity, other-orientation, passivity, gentleness and similar qualities. *Yang* corresponds more to male gender stereotypes like action-orientation, aggression, assertiveness, physical strength and similar attributes. If the gender stereotypes line up with your temperament, all is well. Almost no one is thrown off by a powerful, assertive male who gets things done. In a similar way, almost no one is put off by a sensitive, caring, gentle female who defers to others and nurtures the team. But when we don't have the "right" kinds of traits, people around us are tempted to draw various conclusions about the way we fit in our respective genders.

What happens when these two stereotypes are divergent? In figure 11, you can see that gender divides according to *yin* and *yang*. When our temperament, either introverted or extroverted, is at odds with the gender stereotype normally connected with our sex, we experience another potential layer of cultural rejection.

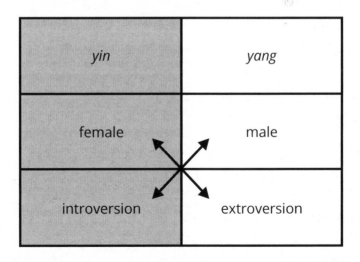

Figure 11. The intersection of gender and temperament.

The arrows in the figure show the potential disconnect between gender and temperament when we cross over the *yin* and *yang* boundary. Being an introverted male or an extroverted high-D ("just do it") female creates an additional potential barrier to group acceptance. While being an outgoing, positive, high-I ("be happy") female is acceptable in Western culture, being a driven woman with a higher D score can be difficult. While being a driven, aggressive, competitive, optimistic, can-do male is acceptable in U.S. culture, being either a high-S ("think about it") or high-C ("do it right") introverted male can be difficult. The alternative to acceptance is rejection.

THE PROBLEM OF REJECTION

One of the things we fear the most, whether the result of gender bias, temperament bias or other factors, is being found outside the inner ring, being left out, rejected. Isn't rejection just a part of life? Shouldn't we just "deal with it" and "get on with life"? Two social psychologists, Mark Leary, whom we met earlier, and Geoff MacDonald, have studied the problem of rejection in depth. They argue that social pain, an emotional reaction to various types of rejection, is just as real as physical pain.[7] All cultures around the world use the language of physical pain to describe social pain. We say things like we were "brokenhearted," "cut to the core," or "emotionally scarred."

Our use of pain language to describe social pain may not just be metaphorical. Recent evidence has suggested a neurological connection between physical pain and emotional or social pain. The same areas of the brain light up in PET scans in relation to both social and physical pain.[8] In addition, certain brain chemicals also point to physiological links between social and physical pain. In other words, social pain likely travels in the same areas of the brain as does physical pain.[9]

Of particular interest to introverts is how our brains appear to process social pain like rejection, marginalization and ostracism.

MacDonald and Leary explained that extroverts and introverts process both kinds of pain differently. Introverts are much more sensitive to rejection and negativity of all types than extroverts. This explains why it is a fallacy to say, "We all experience rejection," as a means of leveling the field. Though we all experience different kinds of rejection leading to social pain, for introverts, the effects of this negativity are multiplied, as shown in figure 12.

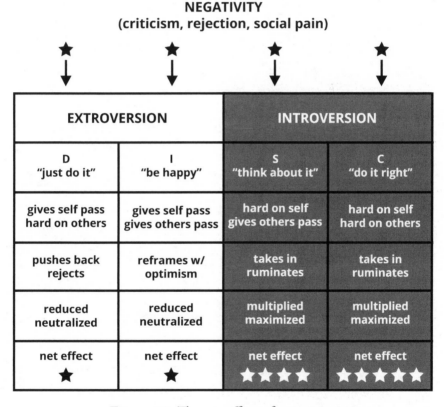

NEGATIVITY
(criticism, rejection, social pain)

EXTROVERSION		INTROVERSION	
D "just do it"	**I** "be happy"	**S** "think about it"	**C** "do it right"
gives self pass hard on others	gives self pass gives others pass	hard on self gives others pass	hard on self hard on others
pushes back rejects	reframes w/ optimism	takes in ruminates	takes in ruminates
reduced neutralized	reduced neutralized	multiplied maximized	multiplied maximized
net effect ★	net effect ★	net effect ★★★★	net effect ★★★★★

Figure 12. The net effect of negativity.

As you can see, introverts tend to multiply the effect of negativity or personal rejection as opposed to extroverts, who tend to either reject it or to reframe it with positivity. High-C introverts, with their focus on doing things right, tend to experience the highest degree of felt rejection in response to themselves or their work being criticized.

All human beings have a basic need to belong. Social exclusion is experienced as a severe threat to our existence. Being out has a detrimental effect on our sense of meaning and overall well-being in the world. For introverts, rejection is even more painful than it is for people with other temperaments.

REFLECTION QUESTIONS

As I reflect on times in my life when I struggled to find meaning, those periods have always been connected to relational loss and social pain. Experiencing the pain of not belonging, not fitting in, not being accepted, has always reduced my ability to derive meaning from life. Consider your own experiences as you reflect on the following questions.

1. Do you remember the in-group in high school? College? Other settings? Were you part of that group or outside of it? How did that feel? What would you have been willing to do to get and stay inside that circle of friends?

2. How would you describe your desire to "belong" in the workplace?

3. Why is belonging so important for all human beings?

4. Can you think of a time when your sense of meaning was diminished as a result of not belonging?

5. Do you fit into typical gender stereotypes? How does your gender contribute or fail to contribute to your sense of belonging?

6. How do you process negativity? Does it seem to hit you harder than extroverts around you?

8

Growth & Loss

"Of all the losses experienced in personal relationships, ambiguous loss is the most devastating because it remains unclear, indeterminate."

—Pauline Boss

Monika grew up in the Midwest. She was the granddaughter of Irish immigrants and had the red hair to prove it. Her days growing up in rural Minnesota were her fondest memories. She was the youngest of eight children and a bit of a surprise to her parents of modest means. After college, she had worked for several years for a software company that "made her feel like she belonged there." In fact, this was really the first place Monika felt at home.

She recounted to me her experiences in grade school of feeling "different." "I was quieter, didn't talk very much, was pretty shy," she told me. "I was sort of a tomboy and dressed more like a boy, didn't feel too comfortable in my own skin." She didn't know quite what made her feel different and suspected that a part of it, at least, was her gender. "I always thought it was about being a girl and that girls were supposed to be and behave a certain way. We were supposed to speak less and not be too aggressive, which was OK with me because I never have felt overly aggressive anyway."

As an adult, Monika was well-read and a bit of a feminist. She identified, as a woman in corporate America, with the problem of the glass ceiling. Her company had other female leaders, though, which gave her hope that maybe the ceiling didn't exist there. Boy, was she wrong!

The new CEO was the stereotype of male aggressive charismatic leadership, the extrovert ideal. He had come from another company that he had just dramatically turned around in three short years and his job now was to do the same or better for Monika's company. He was most definitely a mover and shaker. He perceived her to be a problem from the outset of their relationship. She knew he had issues with "people like her," people whom he perceived as lacking confidence, assertiveness and who weren't outgoing enough, but she was nonetheless surprised at her demotion from her previous leadership position. "I need leaders who are aggressive and optimistic," the CEO explained to her. "You're just not leadership material, at least not in this organization and where I'm taking it."

Monika was devastated. The job she had loved was changing. The place where she had felt like she belonged no longer felt safe. She still had a "job" and tried to be grateful for that, but inside it felt as if the bottom had dropped out of her world. She had invested so many years into the organization and felt like she had been kicked to the curb. She didn't connect the dots at the time to her introversion. Only later would she begin to see the way the CEO's bias against her temperament laid at the base of his decision. It wasn't her gender but her introversion that was used against her as a reason for her demotion. She felt powerless on many levels and deeply sad.

THE LOSSES OF LIFE

Losses like Monika's happen to all of us. The ebb and flow, the *yin* and *yang* of life, the seasons through which we all inevitably pass are normal. So is the normal reaction to those losses, normal sadness. Loss is part and parcel of the human experience. Being connected to people, things or even ideas, all of which are subject to removal from our lives, sets us up for the inevitability of loss. The only way to avoid loss is to avoid being connected to anyone or anything. As C. S. Lewis once famously wrote,

> There is no safe investment. To love at all is to be vulnerable. Love anything, and your heart will certainly be wrung and possibly be broken. If you want to make sure of keeping it intact, you must give your heart to no one, not even to an animal. Wrap it carefully round with hobbies and little luxuries; avoid all entanglements; lock it up safe in the casket or coffin of your selfishness. . . . The alternative to tragedy is damnation. The only place outside Heaven where you can be perfectly safe from all dangers and perturbations of love is Hell.[1]

Lewis was right. To love, to live in connection with others or even our most closely held beliefs, is to make ourselves vulnerable to the inevitability of loss that is inherent in the human experience.

Losses range in size and impact from routine to significant. The research clearly tells us that the most significant losses involve the death of loved ones in our innermost circle. Among these, the most difficult to overcome are the death of a child or spouse. Life, however, also has other losses. Financial catastrophe, bankruptcy or foreclosure can be devastating losses. The failure of a business, the loss of a job and the stigma of unemployment send us reeling.

Some losses are hard to identify. They are ambiguous. The loss of a marriage through divorce for some feels like a death of hopes and dreams. A child of divorce may feel the perceived loss of a parent.

Miscarriage, infertility or other causes of childlessness are losses that our culture struggles to recognize, not knowing how to comfort. The loss of a soldier who never came home from war, the loved ones who were never recovered from 9/11, the emptiness of the nest after the kids fly away, these are all losses complicated by ambiguity.

Growing up as part of the minority, nondominant culture can also be understood as loss. The accident of birth, the situation we find ourselves in from the beginning, for many has facets of ambiguous loss. Introversion in America at the end of the twentieth century, a society intent on promoting extroversion as the definition of psychological health, can be seen as loss. Think of all the stereotypes American, introverted children will have to overcome in their lifetimes. How many positions throughout their working careers will they miss out on due to the presence of an unfair bias that discriminates against them?

We all, from every point along the introvert-extrovert continuum, experience loss. Loss is part of our human experience. As we have seen, some losses are clear to us and others are harder to identify. The loss connected to being an introvert in an extroverted world is real, though most often unacknowledged. The uphill fight for validation is genuine. This loss of the esteem and acceptance of others that brings social pain is not our greatest potential loss, however.

The biggest loss we may suffer is an internal one. When we allow ourselves to believe the message we've been told that we're inadequate, we invalidate ourselves.

MOURNING LOSSES

Our *yang* society is enamored with happiness and fun. The extrovert ideal dominates the landscape. Life is short. Play hard.

This mentality considerably interrupts our ability to grieve well, and many Americans don't know how to mourn. Instead of healthy grief, we often practice unhealthy alternatives. One of our culture's favorite nonsolutions is the attempt to "let it go." As some say, "We all have pain; get over it." Or, we practice denial, "What loss?" Or, we simply numb the pain in unhealthy ways with the use of substances, stimulating experiences or distractions.

We do all these things in the midst of societally accepted losses in our culture, such as the loss of a loved one or a divorce. When someone loses a spouse, we normally give some room for them to grieve, though far less room than is given in other cultures. In Jewish culture, the family sits *shiva*, sitting on low stools and not leaving the home for seven days following a death in the family. A local rabbi recently told me that he has a hard time convincing families in his synagogue to do this today. More proof that Americans don't grieve well.

If losses that we can readily identify often go unmourned, how much more are other losses ignored that are harder to identify or have a cultural stigma attached? "Just as ambiguity complicates loss, it complicates the mourning process," wrote educator and researcher Paulina Boss. "People can't start grieving because the situation is indeterminate. It feels like a loss but it is not *really* one."[2]

Introverts are naturally wired to be good at grief. Most of the philosophers throughout human history have been introverts. They have readily connected with the existential pain around them and contemplated the deep things of life and even the metaphysical. We are, however, living in a world that is upside down sometimes. The sadness we naturally feel is frowned upon, and we are instead given a fresh prescription for more happiness. I agree with Laurie Helgoe, an introvert advocate and psychologist, who can't stand that old Lee Adams song from *Bye Bye Birdie*:

> Pick out a pleasant outlook, stick out that noble chin;
> Wipe off that full-of-doubt look, slap on a happy grin.
> Spread sunshine all over the place
> And just put on a happy, put on a happy,
> Put on a happy face.[3]

Life, real life, not slap-happy life, is a series of positive and negative experiences, seasons of growth and expansion and experiences of loss.

Sometimes we can gain insight by mapping out events in our lives. At www.introvertrevolution.com you'll find a form you can download called "Losses and Gains of Life" on which you can plot the advances and losses of life. Sometimes this exercise can help people get in touch with the losses (and the victories) that have gone before. Review your history and see which losses you perceive as the most significant in your personal development. This historical map may come in handy in the months and years ahead as you continue to process the ups and downs of your life.

THE LOSS OF SADNESS

Our inability to grieve is connected to our cultural obsession with happiness and our growing aversion to depression. In their 2007 book, *The Loss of Sadness: How Psychiatry Transformed Normal Sorrow into Depressive Disorder*, Allan Horwitz and Jerome Wakefield described the process by which modern American culture has lost the concept of normal sadness.[4]

For over 2500 years, going all the way back to Aristotle and continuing until 1980, there was a long-standing tradition of distinguishing between pathological sadness, *melancholia* or *depression*, and *normal sadness*. One of the leading aspects of distinguishing between the two was the connection of normal sadness to a cause, as opposed to depression, which seems to have none. The *with or without cause* distinction has recently been lost in the American mental health industry and is in the process of being lost in the popular culture. As a result of altered diagnostic criteria for a major depressive disorder beginning with the DSM-III in 1980 and continuing to the present, the prevalence of "depression" has been on an exponential rise.

To get a feel for what qualifies as depression, take the following brief survey. Circle the responses that accurately describe your past week.

During the past week . . .	Rarely or none of the time (less than 1 day)	Some of or a little of the time (1–2 days)	Occasionally or a moderate amount of the time (3–4 days)	All of the time (5–7 days)
1. I was bothered by things that usually don't bother me.	0	1	2	3
2. I did not feel like eating; my appetite was poor.	0	1	2	3
3. I felt that I could not shake off the blues even with help from my family.	0	1	2	3
4. I did not feel that I was just as good as other people.	0	1	2	3
5. I had trouble keeping my mind on what I was doing.	0	1	2	3
6. I felt depressed.	0	1	2	3
7. I felt that everything I did was an effort.	0	1	2	3
8. I felt hopeless about the future.	0	1	2	3
9. I thought my life had been a failure.	0	1	2	3
10. I felt fearful.	0	1	2	3
11. My sleep was restless.	0	1	2	3
12. I was unhappy.	0	1	2	3
13. I talked less than usual.	0	1	2	3
14. I felt lonely.	0	1	2	3
15. People were unfriendly.	0	1	2	3
16. I could not enjoy life.	0	1	2	3
17. I had crying spells.	0	1	2	3
18. I felt sad.	0	1	2	3
19. I felt that people disliked me.	0	1	2	3

During the past week . . .	Rarely or none of the time (less than 1 day)	Some of or a little of the time (1–2 days)	Occasionally or a moderate amount of the time (3–4 days)	All of the time (5–7 days)
20. I could not "get going."	0	1	2	3
TOTALS				

Enter your combined total of all (4) columns here _____.

Unless someone close to you died recently, a score of 16 or higher is considered *depressed*. How did you fare? It would be fairly easy to get to 16 by feeling unhappy or sad each day of the week, feeling that people disliked you or were unfriendly each day, and feeling lonely or fearful each day. That's 6 x 3 = 18. You would meet the criteria for depression on the Center for Epidemiologic Studies Depression Scale (CES-D).[5] Worse, if you took this assessment in the context of a counseling relationship, you may have the label "depression" permanently applied to your medical records. If you did score over 16, don't feel bad, many of the self-actualized people on Maslow's list likely would as well.

Things recently got even worse. Just last year, with the issuance of the new DSM-V, the bereavement exclusion for depression had been removed.[6] Now, when you lose a loved one, you'll likely end up with a diagnosis of depression along with the loss. And it probably won't surprise you to learn that things like romantic breakups, losses of jobs, failure to gain an anticipated promotion, disasters, accidents, illness and other ambiguous losses are not factored into the assessment, either.

Our culture, led by the American psychiatric community, the same one that keeps trying to include introversion as diagnosable, has almost successfully eliminated the idea of healthy or normal sadness altogether. Yet what we know from science is that normal sadness in response to losses of all kinds is (1) experienced by not only humans but also by primates, (2) experienced by human infants, (3) a universal feature in all human groups cross-culturally.[7] So, it's normal everywhere in the universe but in America under the thumb of the DSM or in the rest of the world under the jurisdiction of the International Classification of Diseases (ICD).

In a strange mix of data, our rate of depression has increased concurrent with our pursuit of happiness. The more we have moved toward the extrovert ideal (especially the happiness side), the more we have experienced the opposite. Who's borne the brunt of this overdiagnosis? Introverts, who incline more naturally toward the sad side of life, who feel the pain around them and empathize deeply, would be the ones to fail tests like the CES-D and end up with a clinical diagnosis that will follow them in their medical records for the rest of their lives.

Think about Monika, whom we met in the introduction to this chapter. She was sad because she had been wrongly demoted from her previous position, which she enjoyed and which gave her a sense of purpose in the world. She felt like she belonged there and that her work had meaning. Since her demotion, things have been hard. The cause for her sadness is clear: unfair treatment by her boss, the new CEO. And yet, Monika may well end up in a counselor's office receiving a diagnosis so that her insurance company will pay for her treatment. In essence, she gets victimized all over again. This is common in the workplace, the family and all spheres of life.

What will happen if normal sadness is eliminated from our culture? Is this possible? For now, we have only seen or imagined such a society in the fictional account of Stepford.[8] Perhaps in the future, the fantasy of Stepford may become our reality.

REFLECTION QUESTIONS

It is common for introverts in an extroverted world to suffer loss and to experience normal sadness that is sometimes confused with depression. Think about the losses you have suffered connected to your temperament as you answer the following questions.

1. List the five to ten largest losses you have suffered thus far in life.

2. Which of these losses are related to being introverted? How was the extrovert ideal, the perception that you didn't have what it took, a part of these losses?

3. How many of these losses have come at the hands of extroverts? Introverts?

4. As you reflect on these losses, how effectively have you grieved them? Have you had a support system to help you?

5. What has hindered your grieving process?

6. What did you think of your score on the CES-D?

7. What do you think about the DSM-V removal of bereavement as an exclusion for depression? Should this have been done?

8. How is your sadness a normal and healthy response to losses in your life and not pathological depression?

9

Seeing & Feeling

"Sometimes people hold a core belief that is very strong. When they are presented with evidence that works against that belief, the new evidence cannot be accepted. It would create a feeling that is extremely uncomfortable, called cognitive dissonance. And because it is so important to protect the core belief, they will rationalize, ignore and even deny anything that doesn't fit in with the core belief."

—Frantz Fanon

One of the core beliefs many introverts hold is that negative emotions, especially anger, are wrong. Wanting to maintain the unity of the group, we repress our feelings.

"We don't have that bias here," James told me as he thought deeply about the culture of his consulting firm. He had been with the same company for six years and had felt stuck at the director level for the last two years. Though he aspired to become a vice president, the executive leadership couldn't see him in that role. He looked away, then back at me.

"The more I think about it, I do feel frustrated," he hesitantly offered.

"Are you angry?" I asked. "When you think about how they have informed you that you don't have what it takes to be executive leadership, how does it impact you emotionally?"

James was the nicest guy in the world. He was one of those people who would give you the shirt off of his back. He was always quick to advocate for others but struggled to advocate for himself. He was reticent to admit the depth of his feelings about his recent conversation with his supervisor.

"What did she say again?" I asked.

"She said that I wasn't outgoing enough to be a leader. She expressed her concern about my ability to motivate others, that I lacked enthusiasm and the skills needed to really fire up a team."

"How do you feel about that now?"

James has always been a superior performer and managed people and tasks extremely well. While it's true that he's not an over-the-top extrovert, he has wonderful people skills and those who work for him really respect him and know how much he cares.

"I'm frustrated."

"Would you say you're angry?"

"No, just irritated."

It was then that I knew we were going to be doing the I'm-angry-but-I'm-uncomfortable-admitting-it dance. Introverts often use words like "frustrated" or "irritated" instead of the word "angry." I often help them see that frustration and irritation are in the anger family. They're actually angry, just not comfortable admitting it to themselves or others.

"It's not that bad, really. I'm just oversensitive. I'm sure it's just me. It'll be fine, I'm sure," James said.

Contrast James with Kate. Kate is a highly successful executive in the software industry. She clearly sees the bias against introverts and is in touch with her emotional reaction to it. Here's what she had to say when I interviewed her about the effects of being discriminated against or misjudged as an introvert.

"I feel like I'm unfairly treated all the time. I have to meet extroverted people face-to-face to even get to be listened to. I feel like extroverted people bulldoze introverted people. If you don't speak up, they assume you have nothing to say. It is freaking annoying."

"Do you think the extrovert bias is real, or am I just paranoid?"

"I feel so unfairly treated. Especially in America, there is a real bias. It's absolutely out there."

"How do you feel about being treated this way? Does it ever make you mad?"

"It only makes me mad if it crosses my values and boundaries. For example, if they think that I am incompetent and show their contempt in their actions, that is annoying."

Kate and James are at different places in terms of seeing and feeling the impact of the extrovert ideal around them. Kate feels what she feels because she allows herself to see.

SEEING

What we don't see can't hurt us, or so we tell ourselves. In large part due to *yang* influences, our culture is among the greatest in history at suppressing painful realities all around us. We are a culture in denial, pretending that bad, painful or scary things just don't exist. This contributes to the problems we have with healthy grieving, as we explored in the last chapter. Our happiness culture sets us up for failure when it comes to seeing the ubiquity of painful things around us. If we don't see pain, we won't have to experience the feelings that would result from noticing it.

Introverts as collectivists can easily fall into this pattern of denial. We tend to think first and sometimes almost exclusively of others. We tend not to like conflict because it represents a clear threat to our desire for togetherness. Introverts enjoy nothing more than everyone being in harmony with one another. When things are even slightly discordant, it can trigger an unhealthy dynamic in us. We conspire to conceal reality, hiding our true feelings. We work extra hard to keep everyone from seeing the dysfunction all around us so as to preserve a sense of unity, even if it is false. We even seek to suppress those feelings from our own awareness. If we pretend we don't see dysfunction, we will have nothing to feel negative emotions about and the team will stay intact.

Extroverts are different. They are much more comfortable with anger, a negative emotion, and with expressing it. When things aren't right, generally they'll let others around them know. What seems strange to us as introverts is the remarkable ability of extroverts to quickly get over their anger and to move on. We can have a run-in with them in the morning, and only a few hours later, they are over it, wanting to go to lunch together. It's typically not like this for introverts. We're more like elephants. We never forget, at least not without a clear process of working things through to closure.

This whole strategy of pretending is ineffective in the end because it doesn't solve our inner angst. For this reason, many introverts are walking around with lists of things that have happened to us in the past. Because we so often fail to tell others how they have offended us, we deprive ourselves of the means to resolve past conflicts.

Though we try not to see, we do. Are you seeing the situation as it is in your world? Can you see the cultural influences and biases that affect you and your workplace on a daily basis? Will you allow yourself to? Or are you hindered by your concern for the well-being and harmony of the rest of the team around you? Once we begin to be honest with ourselves about what we see, we may also begin to feel more deeply in response.

FEELING

How comfortable are you with acknowledging, owning or expressing your feelings? Many introverts are masters at projecting a different face to those around them than the rich and complex emotional life they are really feeling inside.[1] Introverts are often poker-faced and can be very hard to read by others. Our excessive other-orientation causes us to defer to the will of others in the moment and then sometimes to struggle with resentment following.

We so often claim that "all is well," that "we're fine," when it is not true; we have actually become disconnected from our own feelings. We can even begin to believe the lies we tell others. Can we allow ourselves to feel emotions that connect with this reality, or will we allow ourselves and the culture of happiness around us to invalidate our true feelings? Is feeling our true feelings important?

There are many theories of emotion and just as many lists of primary emotions. *Primary emotions* are those core emotions that cannot be combined with or described by any other emotions. All emotions can be seen as flowing from these primary emotions. Phillip Shaver is a psychologist who focuses on the areas of attachment theory and emotions, how we connect and how it makes us feel. Shaver et al. listed the following primary emotions: *love, joy, surprise, anger, sadness* and *fear*.[2] These basic emotions as part of the healthy human condition are defined as follows:

- Love: healthy, other-oriented response

- Joy: healthy response to the good things in life

- Surprise: healthy response to unexpected information or events

- Anger: healthy response to boundaries or standards being violated

- Sadness: healthy response to loss or pain

- Fear: healthy response to threat or danger

All other emotions flow out of these six basic emotions or are combinations and variations on these themes.

Emotional intelligence (EQ) is intimately connected to our ability to deeply understand and apply the full spectrum of healthy varieties of human emotion inside us. The foundational skill of EQ, self-awareness, is the ability to rightly identify what we are feeling in response to life as it unfolds around us, to be honest with ourselves.

In many ways, due to our inward disposition and natural introspectiveness, introverts are extremely well suited to developing this kind of healthy self-awareness. We're paying close attention to what's happening and tend to feel things very deeply. The difficulty comes, in part, from the culture around us, the fishbowl we live in. It sometimes discourages us from openly expressing our *yin* emotions. So, we suppress them. Affirming the validity of our true feelings, both *yin* and *yang*, is a key part of our movement toward authenticity as leaders.

YIN AND *YANG* EMOTIONS

We can sort Shaver's list of primary emotions into two lists that tend to be associated with either side of the *yin yang* construct as illustrated in figure 13.

Figure 13. *Yin* and *yang* emotions.

As you can see, two of the six primary emotions naturally connect to the pattern of introversion; they are *yin*. Introverts incline more toward sadness and fear. Three of the six connect more naturally to extroversion; they are *yang*. Extroverts tend to flow innately toward joy, anger and surprise, which are connected to change. Remember in the *yin yang* metaphor, there is a drop of each in the other. In reality, we all experience all six core emotions in different ways, at different times and in varying degrees.

Love seems to be the exception. It is related to the universal human need for belonging and is a core need for introverts and extroverts alike. We all need to be loved and to express love to others in order to be healthy. Examining these six emotions from the perspective of introversion will allow us to learn how to own all of our feelings and move toward our full humanity.

We begin on the *yin* side. Introverts quite naturally feel *sadness*. It goes with the temperament. We are wired to be more aware of troubling things around us in the world. As we discussed in the previous chapter, healthy sadness is at risk of being written out of the cultural narrative. And yet for most of recorded history, human society has understood and accepted the reality of sorrow as part of being fully human.

Healthy people cry in times of sorrow and in times of great joy. We even cry when triggered by onions. Researchers have studied people's tears and found that different types of tears have different structures.[3] Though producing structurally different tears, perhaps these two emotions, sadness and happiness, are more intrinsically interconnected than some would have us believe. Being able to experience normal sadness is a healthy strength of introversion.

Introverts also tend to deal with more *fear*. They are frequently afraid of making mistakes, afraid of disrupting the unity of the team, afraid of too much risk, and sometimes afraid of change. They tend to be more realistic or pessimistic and are highly skilled at seeing the problems with situations, plans and strategies. While extroverts tend to live in the present, introverts tend to live in the past and the future. The past reminds us of mistakes and bad outcomes, giving us a healthy fear of repeating them. By projecting outcomes into the future, we more readily see impending danger and feel the motivating effect of fear that helps us avoid it.[4] Though it is most often framed as a liability in a *yang* culture, healthy fear can actually be an emotional asset.

Similarly to the way sadness is being removed from the culture, normal fear is also under attack. What we used to see as normal healthy fear is now increasingly being viewed through the lens of pathology as anxiety and neurosis. Since 1980, the rules have been changed. By using current standards, we now assess that over half of the entire population will suffer from an anxiety disorder at some point in their lives, a rate twenty times higher than it was prior to the change in criteria.[5]

In light of the cultural bias, is it a surprise that these two main *yin* emotions of sadness and fear would be not only marginalized but pathologized? Our *yang* culture has sought, perhaps unintentionally, to all but eradicate these two "negative emotions" from human experience. Wouldn't life be better without sadness or fear? Western culture suggests yes. Horwitz and Wakefield, the social scientists we met in the previous chapter, rightly criticized this view by saying, "Pathology cannot be equated with the sheer presence of negative emotions, since bad feelings can often exist for good reasons and be normal."[6]

The potential loss of these *yin* emotions would constitute a significant loss. Many advantages in life are connected to our ability to experience the full range of human emotions, even the ones sometimes called "negative."[7] Many advantages spring from the dark side of our emotional humanity that includes distress tolerance, the ability to tolerate psychological discomfort en route to our growth and development.

The *yang* definition of the good life is a life of happiness or *joy*. Joy is a positive emotion related to a sense of euphoria and contentment usually derived from pleasant and fulfilling experiences. Introverts, contrary to popular myth, experience plenty of this *yang* emotion, though it tends to look a bit different sometimes, causing some extroverts to wonder if we're really happy at all. Our introverted joy is often less enthusiastic or expressive. It may be a quieter and different kind of happiness. In fact, we each may have different set points for happiness that align with our different temperaments.[8] Nonetheless, just as the extroverts around us, we also desire and experience many moments and seasons of joy in our journey. But joy needs the other contrasting emotions to be what it was intended, light in contrast to darkness.

Anger is another characteristic emotion on the *yang* side. Introverts tend to under-anger. We have long fuses allowing us to put up with a lot before we reach a breaking point. If we do break and express anger, most of us feel disproportionately bad about what we may have said or felt in the heat of the moment. We just aren't comfortable with this emotion that can be an important part of our full humanity.

Healthy anger is a signal that a boundary has been crossed, that something wrong has been done. It connects to our sense of justice or fairness, something many introverts feel deeply. For introverts, we may need to give ourselves permission to feel justified anger toward not only the injustices committed against others but toward those committed against us. Being angry may be quite healthy, especially as we begin to initially understand the cultural biases, myths and unfairness connected to the promotion of the extrovert ideal.

Surprise is the result of experiencing the unexpected. It is related to change, something extroverts like. Introverts, on the other hand, tend to like things being more predictable. If change is needed, we will normally better accept it with adequate time to process its coming. Surprise may never truly feel good to us. We don't need or crave the additional adrenaline or dopamine that comes from being surprised. While we may not like surprises or the feelings they engender, there is one thing we all need, extrovert and introvert alike.

We all need *love*, to feel love, to be loved and accepted, to belong. This is directly connected to our sense of well-being and meaning in the world. Love is the connecting point for introverts and extroverts, our common need and the means by which we can move together toward a sense of balance (*he*). Embracing differences and loving each other not only despite but also because of those differences is the means by which we together can move toward the ideal society. Once loved in this way, we are enabled to feel love toward others.

To feel all six of these emotions—sadness, fear, joy, anger, surprise and love—in the context of a full life is the goal. Though these emotions are often referred to as positive or negative, in reality, they are all healthy aspects of being fully human and can only be determined to be good or bad in context.

Rather than emphasizing one side, typically *yang*, at the expense of the other, typically *yin*, the whole person can move toward what some have called *emodiversity*.[9] Psychologist Jordi Quoidbach gave the following example. Person A experiences three moments of joy in a given day. Person B experiences two moments of joy and one of contentment. Person C experiences two moments of joy and one of anxiety. Can we simply add up the positives and subtract the negatives to determine which person is happiest (well-adjusted)? This is precisely the way the math is being done today. Instead, Quoidbach and his colleagues have suggested that emodiversity, a variety of and abundance of rich emotional experiences from across the full spectrum, is what characterizes a life lived well. Emodiversity sees an upside in both our dark (*yin*) and light (*yang*) emotional aspects of life.[10]

Seeing the reality around us and giving ourselves permission to feel our emotional response is key to our personal revolution as introverts. Realizing that our culture is attempting to measure many aspects of our natural selves with the wrong ruler is crucial. Fully embracing our emotional selves, with our natural strengths toward deeply feeling sadness and fear, is necessary to our journey toward self-acceptance. Giving ourselves permission to feel appropriately healthy anger is crucial. Emotions, all of them, play an organizing rather than a disruptive role in human functioning. They are biologically adaptive. They move us. They inform us. They motivate us to action.[11]

Forbes writer Jenna Goudreau was surprised at the response she received from her January 26, 2012, piece, "The Secret Power of Introverts." Introverts commented to her in droves. One, in particular, described the full range of emotions connected to the current cultural plight of introverts.

> I am not sure whether to laugh or cry. . . . Therein lies the rub of being an introvert: a world that values chattiness and socialization, even in the workplace, I find suffocating and at times traumatizing.[12]

Is this reader being overly dramatic? Or is this situation sometimes and in some ways traumatizing? Our feelings, if allowed to find expression, may help us determine the answers to these questions.

REFLECTION QUESTIONS

Introverts tend to not give themselves permission to fully feel a wide range of emotions. How about you? Reflect on your own journey as you answer the following questions.

1. What aspects of your mistreatment as an introvert are you trying not to see? How's that working for you?

2. What feelings about being introverted have you tried not to feel?

3. What are you afraid will happen if you feel what you're trying not to?

4. Of the six primary emotions, which are most difficult for you to feel? Why?

5. How are you with anger? How comfortable are you with expressing it when necessary? What happens when you suppress your anger?

6. How comfortable are you with expressing sadness? Fear? Why?

7. How do you handle surprises? Do you like or dislike the feelings that come when you are surprised? Why?

8. How much joy do you have in your life currently? Why?

9. Do you need to be loved? To feel love? Why or why not?

10. Why is *emodiversity* an important concept?

10

Shame & Detox

"Shame is the experience of being fundamentally bad as a person. Nothing you have done is wrong, and nothing you can do will make up for it. It is a total experience that forbids communication with words."

—Gershen Kaufman

As I sat down to talk, I could feel the pain in Walt. The situation he had recently faced began to surface as we spoke. Just two weeks prior, he had been given difficult news that his position and security within the organization he had served for many years were now uncertain. This was due not to his work performance but to the perception that his leadership style "may not work with where the organization is going," as a higher-up had commented.

"Yes, a sense of loss," he said. "I feel sad and mad. The anger comes from thinking that someone can make a decision based on second-hand information like that. . . .To have somebody of influence say that my career might be better pursued somewhere else—very frustrating and disappointing."

"This stereotype of leadership seems to be having a powerful impact on you."

"It gives me the reality check that there are certain career ladders I will never climb. I've been told as much. There are certain levels to which an introverted leader is well suited. Sometimes, because of cultural expectations, whether I'm well suited or not, those opportunities will not be given to me."

Earlier in the interview, I had asked Walt when he had first become aware of his introversion.

"I remember some instances as clearly as if I had just lived them," he responded. "I was in fifth grade. I came from a very poor family. If your pants tore at the knee, your mom sewed a patch on. You didn't get new pants. For whatever reason, the day I wore those pants to school, it was art class and my teacher needed an art subject. She put a chair up on top of the table and I sat on that chair. I sat with my hands firmly on my knees for the full half hour or however long it was, feeling very shy, very embarrassed. I probably blushed the whole time."

"What would you have called it then?"

"That I was shy."

Walt felt embarrassment and shame about his pants and his family's socioeconomic status, which was exacerbated by being put on display. Under the gaze of all of his classmates, he felt exposed. Knowing how introverts experience social pain and rejection, you can imagine just how painful it was for him that day.

"What other recollections do you have about feeling shy or different?"

"When I was younger, I thought there was something wrong with me. I completely thought there was something wrong with me. Why can't I be comfortable in this situation? . . . uhhhh [painful pause] There were days I was sad, days I was mad, days I couldn't figure out why I just couldn't change and be more like them. Why do I have to be the one who is petrified to go up in front of the class to solve a math problem? So, for a long time I did think there was something wrong with me. Going through relationships as I got older, thinking there were things wrong with me because people around me were telling me that there were things wrong with me."

"Was it only like this at school? How was it at home?"

"I could never live up to my parents' expectations. I could never do things right. I felt like there was something wrong with me, everywhere, at home and at school."

Shame from within and without, the cumulative effect of all the negative feedback in Walt's life was a dull sense of "something's wrong with me." Walt, at a deep but unspoken level, felt worthless, unlovable and somehow inherently flawed as a human being. He hesitated to speak openly about what he felt about himself and had probably been keeping it secret for most of his adult life.

Talking more honestly in recent months about his private feelings has started to change the dynamic somewhat. Lately, Walt is starting to question the gremlin's message about his worth. "Gremlins" are what Brené Brown calls the little voices in our head that speak shame over us. Walt was learning some effective techniques to expose the shame in his life, to bring it out into the light with trustworthy friends and watch its power and authority begin to dissipate. Beginning to deal with the core problem of shame is giving Walt renewed hope for a brighter future. This is a key part of the journey toward wholeness as a leader for many introverts.

TWO ASPECTS OF SADNESS

In the previous chapter, we talked about the need to understand and feel our emotions, both *yin* and *yang*, as a significant part of being fully human. Thus far, we've talked only about the six primary emotions. We noted the attempts in our culture to eliminate normal sadness, the kind that naturally connects to losses of all sorts. If we drill down one level further into sadness, we can identify two critical subtypes of sadness we often feel as introverts. Differentiating between these two is critical for our ongoing well-being, development and leadership.

The first of these is the emotion called *guilt*. Guilt, in the sadness family, is always experienced as a negative thing. It's painful. The feeling of guilt reminds us we have done something wrong and moves us toward action to repair the damage. The action tendency is to atone, to make things right.[1] Healthy or true guilt is an aspect of a functioning conscience, a moral thermometer. This normally healthy emotion can go awry in the life of an introvert, however. The consciences of introverts (especially high C) are very active, perhaps overactive. Doing the right thing and complying with the rules are things many introverts tend to take very seriously. When we don't do things perfectly, we can be relentless in beating ourselves up over our imperfection.

This inner turmoil and self-blaming can lead to a phenomenon known as false guilt. *False guilt* feels like real or true guilt, but it is not based on actual wrongdoing. It is usually connected with being over-responsible, a trait many introverts struggle with. The good news about false guilt is that it is false. When the facts are examined more closely, it disappears. Perfection was never possible; honest mistakes and omissions happen. True guilt is based on actual wrongdoing; false guilt is based on misinformation. Aside from the harmful phenomenon of false guilt, guilt is a healthy functional human emotion that motivates us to correct situations and relationships.

The other relevant subtype of human sadness, however, is a different story. *Shame* is another emotion on the tree of sadness. It is always toxic. When it's in the water you swim in, it will eventually kill you.

SHAME: THE TOXIN

Rejection and other forms of negativity happen to us and outside of us. Shame occurs from internalizing those external messages. It is common for introverts in an extroverted society to develop higher levels of shame connected to a general sense of "something is wrong with me." To get a sense of the toxicity of your inner life, answer the following true/false questions.

1.	I have a hard time believing that introverts can be great leaders.	T or F
2.	I often feel like there is something wrong with me related to my introversion.	T or F
3.	I often wish I was more extroverted.	T or F
4.	I am painfully aware of my introversion at times.	T or F
5.	I have been told that I have poor eye contact, slump my shoulders or blush easily. [1]	T or F
6.	When I make mistakes, I feel bad for hours, even days.	T or F
7.	I fear I don't have what it takes to be a good leader.	T or F
8.	I often feel like an imposter.	T or F
9.	My _____ disqualifies me from being a leader.	T or F
10.	If people really knew me, they wouldn't like me.	T or F

The more questions you responded to as true, the higher the level of shame you are feeling connected to your introversion. There may be lots of things floating in your water that are harmful to you. Like algae and other contaminants in the water of an aquarium, you may have allowed these toxins to build up in your tank.

The most deadly thing in your head is shame. What is shame? Guilt is the sense (sometimes healthy, other times not) that I've *done* something wrong. Shame says, "I *am* something wrong" or "there's something wrong with *me*." Shame is taking the rejection we experience outwardly and adding an inward component. We, in effect, reject ourselves. Shame tells us that we are unworthy of love and belonging, that we are inherently and fundamentally flawed and that the group is right to cast us out.[3]

Shame is personal and interpersonal. It condemns us internally and it involves feeling exposed or naked before the eyes of others. We feel looked down upon by others and feel their contempt and disgust. Because of this, shame is always connected to a desire to hide.[4] We want to disappear, to be invisible.

At the heart of what many introverts feel in an extroverted world is shame. It can be hard to identify and prefers not to be. It thrives in darkness and secrecy. If you listen carefully, however, you may hear it in your inner dialogue and in the thoughts and opinions of others around you. Whether coming from others or from inside you, this is what shame sounds like:

- If people really knew you, they wouldn't like you.

- You're an imposter. You're not an expert at anything.

- You don't have what it takes to be an executive leader here.

- You'll never move up in this organization.

- You're not what we're looking for.

- What's wrong with you? Why can't you be more _____?

- [After brainstorming session] Why couldn't you come up with something? What's wrong with you?

- We need people with _____. You're just not _____.

Are these comments and questions being expressed to you or floating through your head? How often do these kinds of thoughts paralyze you and hinder you from greater confidence, creativity and transparency? Do you feel shame in your body, your face or ears become hot, blush, sweat, or experience time slowing down as you reflect on this reality and read the previous statements?

Interestingly, the bodily symptoms of shame are the same as those of trauma. Shame, in other words, is a traumatic experience.[5] It often involves blushing, time slowing down, ears becoming hot, and other physical manifestations that are identical to those we experience when the limbic system (the fight, flight or freeze system) takes over in the midst of traumatic experiences. It is very real and something we need to learn to defend ourselves from if we're going to move toward becoming the leaders we want to be. How we do fight back against shame?

SHAME DEFENSES

If shame is such a toxic substance, wouldn't it be good for us simply not to ingest it? "Just don't let it into your heart or mind," someone might suggest. "Don't let it get to you." "Shake it off." This is where a deeper understanding of introversion helps to understand why this simplistic strategy won't necessarily work. Extroverts and introverts have different susceptibility to the damaging effects of shame in relation to our rejection sensitivity, as discussed earlier.[6] When someone, or even the culture in general, gives us a shaming message, we all follow different paths of reacting to that toxic information.

When negative comments, feedback or criticism is dropped into the head of a high-D extrovert, they immediately fight back. They have a natural protective tendency that pushes back when pushed. For the high-I extrovert, it's a bit different. They see the world as positive and are optimistic about the worst that life can throw at them. Though they like to be liked by others and might feel a tinge of rejection in hearing negative feedback, their natural optimism kicks in and reframes the content in a much more positive light. They just won't let it get them down.

Contrast introverts. High-S introverts hear the negative comments about themselves or their work and take it in. It resonates too much. High-C introverts listen to the criticism or shame and let it sink down deep into their minds and hearts. They are already acutely aware of their own imperfections and this new data is consistent with the inner critic, their superego, which already speaks loudly in their heads. Introverts have fewer natural defenses against the damaging intruder of shame. If allowed, it will come in and wreak havoc in our minds. Once its effects are deeply felt and experienced over time, we are in need of detox.

DETOX & RESILIENCE

As you can imagine, swallowing that kind of poison, especially over months or years, can have deadly effects on someone. A few of the introverts I have interviewed have experienced very little shaming. The number of introverts who have gone through this cultural experience unscathed is, however, quite small. Most of us on the introverted side feel at least low levels of shame connected to our introversion. Some of us feel it more acutely. Whatever our current level of shame, there is nothing more critical to moving forward as an authentic leader than learning how to detox from its deadly effects.

Detox from controlled and controlling substances can be a dangerous thing. When someone detoxes from alcohol, medical supervision is needed. It is similar with detox from shame. Coincidentally, one of the most common ways we deal with shame is through the use of numbing. To do this, we only have a few options. We can use escape mechanisms of various kinds (alcohol, prescription or nonprescription drugs, other addictions, entertainment, workaholism, etc.). Maybe you can begin to see how shame traps us. It pushes us toward unhealthy coping mechanisms to numb the pain it brings and then leaves us feeling worse and more ashamed as a result of our numbing strategy of choice. The downward cycle continues.

How do we break this cycle and move toward lower levels of shame? It begins with seeing it.

Shame is the topic no one wants to talk about. I suspect this is the reason why so few hands are raised when I ask an audience how many are introverts. The secret about shame is that it relies on secrecy. What it can't tolerate is the light, exposure. Brené Brown has identified three incredibly powerful and helpful things about shame. She calls these the Shame 1-2-3s:[7]

1. We all have shame.

2. We're all afraid to talk about it.

3. The less we talk about it, the more powerful it is.

Though we all have shame, I believe introverts have it in larger doses. In addition, the power of shame itself tends to be greater in the heart of an introvert. Breaking the grip of shame begins by talking about it. It's counterintuitive, but the way out of shame is vulnerability. Jessica Van Vliet is a shame researcher who has developed a theory of shame resilience, a way to work through shame, as a result of in-depth interviews with research participants. Her theory involves five aspects:[8]

1. *Connecting* with others who are safe. This is counterintuitive to the deceptive logic of shame that seeks to make us isolated. We can't and shouldn't be vulnerable with just anybody but only those who have proven themselves to be true. It is the presence of the caring empathetic other, even if they don't say anything but simply sit with us in our shame, that is crucial.[9] Their presence suggests that they are saying, "me, too."

2. *Refocusing* our attention on the whole person we are. This involves rebalancing our attention by focusing on positive aspects of self, not just the negative. Seeing that we, like everybody else, have a mixture of good and bad qualities normalizes our experience and helps us to de-catastrophize it.

3. *Accepting* the reality of the situation and the shame we are feeling. Avoiding the tendency to minimize or to go into denial will allow us to alter our relationship with shame. Acknowledging shame, saying its lies out loud and bringing it out into the open gives us new power over it.

4. *Understanding* the external factors involved and separating shame from ourselves. This involves calling shame out, exposing it for what it is. It is not us. The truth about who we are and the lies of shame can be differentiated. We can begin to distinguish the two different voices.

5. *Resisting* negative judgments about the self. This involves pushing back against shame, challenging its claims about us. Challenging the logic of shame allows us to see the lies on which it rests.

By following a similar process of practicing shame resilience with safe others who will sit with us in our shame, over time and through repetition, we can begin to break the debilitating power of shame in our lives. For me, those safe others have at times been professional counselors. At many other times, it has been my wife, my sister or a few carefully selected friends who can listen to me, even in shame, and remain empathically connected to me. I also have the privilege of being the safe other for many people. Finding your safe others is crucial.

Reducing the detrimental effects of accumulated shame is a key to future development as an introverted leader. Shame is a deadly toxin and too often is dumped on us and into us by difficult people in our environment. Some people around us have bad habits. They have fallen into a repetitive pattern that uses shame as their primary way to motivate others. Many of these difficult people fall on the extroverted end of the spectrum.

DEALING WITH DIFFICULT PEOPLE

One introvert recently asked me, "So, why do we (introverts) always have to do all of the adapting? Why don't the high-D extroverts around us ever have to change?" Dealing with the cultural stereotypes, some of which we have internalized, is bad enough. But what do you do with difficult people in your workplace who can make life "hell" for an introvert?

Particularly difficult for introverts in the workplace are the extroverts around and above them. To be fair, it's not just extroverts, but mostly extroverts who "don't get it."[10] These people are a lethal cocktail for introverts. How can you cope? How can you better manage these difficult people and situations? Here are some particularly useful skills to help you better relate with difficult extroverts around you:

- *Be assertive*. Sometimes, assertiveness is confused with aggressiveness. Most introverts move to the opposite end of the spectrum, passivity. In reality, the middle point of assertiveness is very helpful for introverts dealing with extroverts. Being assertive means finding your voice, expressing your thoughts, feelings and opinions in a way that suits your individual temperament. Feeling better about your introversion and reducing levels of shame will help you do this.

- *Have clear boundaries*. This goes hand in hand with assertiveness. People with good boundaries do not readily get imposed or put upon. They have learned to say both yes and no to requests made of them. Many introverts, due to other-orientation, struggle with maintaining good boundaries with extroverts. Draw upon the drop of *yang* inside you to make your boundaries clear to others.

- *Be more decisive.* This is not to say you should try to be a high-D extrovert. Rather, try not to be overly indecisive in the presence of difficult people. Work through your own doubts, make the best decision you can, and present your answer or solution without wavering or being overly humble or self-effacing (these look like weakness to difficult people). Be vulnerable with someone safe after the meeting but not with the person you struggle with. Don't over-share or be overly transparent.

- *Minimize exposure.* Stop hoping things will get better. Face the reality that some extroverts in your circles are probably not going to understand you nor are they going to adapt their behavior to better relate to you. You may simply need to limit contact with people who have an ongoing detrimental effect on you. Realize that continued exposure to shame and other forms of negativity is toxic.

In these ways, you can identify, expose, reduce and minimize the ongoing external sources of shame in your life. Fortunately, not all extroverts are of this ilk. Many extroverts will understand the dynamic between you and them and will adapt from their side as you adapt from yours. Whatever you do, you must learn to effectively deal with shame in your life, to prevent its toxin from penetrating to your core being as a leader. Shame is the low point on our journey as introverted leaders.

REFLECTION QUESTIONS

Unfortunately, I know from personal experience the pain of the debilitating effects of shame. Carefully consider the following questions. (If it is too painful to consider these questions, consider making an appointment with a counselor, another caring professional or a close friend to help you process through them.)

1. What were you feeling as you read this chapter?

2. How does your shame connect to your introversion?

3. What do you feel ashamed about? What are the shame messages in your head?

4. How do you differentiate shame and guilt?

5. How toxic is your inner dialogue? How much shame are you hearing and feeling inside?

6. What safe people do you have in your life you can begin to practice shame resilience with?

7. What people in your life are ongoing sources of toxic shame? What can you do to minimize or eliminate the damage to you?

PART THREE

Retaking the Stage

"They have their exits and their entrances."

—William Shakespeare

Part two deepened our understanding of previous life experiences and the impact they have had on us as people and leaders. We learned that who we have become is a combination of our inborn temperament and the nurture or lack of nurture we have experienced since childhood. We've begun to get in touch with our losses related to introversion, see the biases, and feel the full spectrum of feelings in response. We've examined the possibility of deeper damage in the form of shame and are beginning to detox from its effects. Now we're ready to step forward and lead in a new way.

In part three, we look at retaking the stage. This time the script is different. Instead of reading lines that don't feel right, you get to read lines that feel like things you would naturally say. This time you're typecast as an introverted leader playing an introverted leader, not a stereotype of an introvert but a real introvert with all the natural yin *strengths that go with it, leading with confidence and authenticity as yourself. On your journey, you move from working through the past to facing the future. What is it that you have been placed on this planet to do?*

To do this, it will require a personal revolution of sorts. You and I, we will have to revolt against a cultural bias fueled by false myths and stereotypes. We'll have to revolt against systemic rejection, even at low levels, that may have led to feelings of shame. We'll need to revolt against the idea of positive psychology and embrace our emodiversity without apology.

Each of us has had a unique experience of being yin *in a* yang *world, and we each follow a unique path back toward wholeness and confidence as leaders. The way forward isn't really stages or steps but the repeated application and practice of new habits of thinking, feeling, doing and being. We may find ourselves back at earlier stages of cultural identity development due to discovering new information or having another encounter with an extrovert who invalidates us. Setbacks are to be expected. Our task, however, is to get up each time we fall back and to continue to push forward toward greater levels of authenticity. In doing so, we will develop the kind of leadership those we serve desperately need.*

11

Rejection & Acceptance

"Those who make peaceful revolution impossible will make violent revolution inevitable."

—John F. Kennedy

When I was in my first class in a counseling program, I was pretty unaware, clueless really, of the reality of biases inside me. I remember my professor, Dr. Thuerer, who was an adjunct on loan from the college across town and very different than me in his political ideology and worldview. He seemed to see and push all of my buttons, which were obvious to him even though I didn't recognize them myself.

The class he taught was multicultural counseling. He assigned us optional reading in Ronald Takaki's *A Different Mirror: A History of Multicultural America*. That book and Dr. Thuerer made a big impact on my life. For the first time, I was exposed to new realizations like the following:

- The way Native Americans were dehumanized and dispossessed by the "Christian" settlers who claimed a divine sanction to take their land.

- How the slave trade developed, dehumanizing Africans for centuries prior to the history of slavery in America.

- The way the Irish were pushed out of their land by the British.

- How Mexicans were pushed out of the western United States, including California, the state I was born and raised in.

- The many ways Chinese people were taken advantage of in the construction of the West and of the railroads.

- The widespread nature of anti-Semitism around the world.

- How over 127,000 Japanese were placed in internment camps in the United States during WWII.[1]

- The way the civil rights struggle in the U.S. actually happened, including the murder of Emmett Till and other horrific events.

- The unfair way that women and children have been treated as less than men throughout most of history.

I began to realize that I had been taught a revised history as told through the lens of white male American stereotypes and biases. I vividly remember feeling ashamed for the first time that I was white, that I was male, and that I was somehow connected or related to the people behind these historical atrocities. The more I thought and reflected on the other side of the historical story, the angrier I got. I was furious that I had not been given all of the facts and allowed to draw my own conclusions.

We can't reject what we don't see or acknowledge. Once I began to see the whole story of American history, my views of things began to change.

I suspect it's that way for each of us as we begin to see the reality of the cultural biases connected to introversion. Many of us have experienced rejection connected to our temperament. These myths have caused us social pain and may even have led to shame inside, but while we felt that rejection, we didn't have the whole picture, a full view of *why* we were being rejected. The first step out of the past is a step of rejection. It may sound counterintuitive, but we need to reject our rejection.

Walt from the last chapter finds himself at a crossroads. If he allows these negative messages and stereotypes to govern how he sees himself, he'll play right into the hand of his new supervisor. He needs to reject the messaging, the shame and the false version of himself that is connected to these two. "Who you are is fine," he says to himself. "Don't let her define you. Don't hide your true self." Walt is in the process of gaining brand new levels of self-acceptance. He's learning to accept his temperament and gaining new skills to more effectively manage situations as an introvert. He's learning his limits. Simply rejecting the negative is not enough; it must be accompanied by a positive acceptance of the good of introversion for sustained change to take place.

REJECTING THE NEGATIVE

Sometimes rejection can be a good thing. Rejecting ideas, particularly false or destructive ideas, can be a life-giving and invigorating thing. There are three key aspects of healthy rejection we need to practice.

First, we need to *reject the cultural messaging* that perpetuates the status quo. Throughout this book, we've shown the reality of the extrovert ideal in the West. No place is this problem more painful or detrimental than in the American workplace. Leaders, especially introverted ones, are told all kinds of misinformation about themselves and their supposed inadequacies. On a cultural or organizational level, what can we do about it? While one person can't change an entire system and heal its dysfunctions, you can do small things to disrupt the system. Here are some ways you can be a catalyst for change in your environment:

- Educate others on, and raise awareness of, the reality of introversion and the prevalence of the extrovert ideal. Debunk the myths that many on the team are still holding about you, themselves or others.

  o Pass on relevant articles you read about introversion.

  o Give a copy of this or similar books to teammates.

  o Gently correct misconceptions and stereotypes when you hear them.

  o Do a lunch-and-learn training with teammates on the subject of introversion.

- Support other introverts on the team with encouragement, understanding and nurture.

- Talk to your direct supervisor about how best to manage or motivate you or other introverts in your organization.

- Be an example of a healthy, self-aware introverted leader.

If shame is the low point in our journey, the *rejection of shame* marks the beginning of our way upward. The greatest enemy we face on this journey toward authenticity is shame. It is the driving force behind so much of the propensity we have to shrink back and return to the shadows where we cannot be seen. If we do not reject shame, we cannot be innovative. Creativity is killed by the specter of shame. I feel this powerful force every time I undertake a new writing project. "This is no good," shame says. "Who do you think you are? You're not a real author. Who would ever buy this book?" We can see how rejecting shame is essential to being our authentic selves and to stepping up toward that ultimate purpose for which we exist.

Thirdly, we need to reject the *false self* we have manufactured as a result of cultural messaging and fear of exposure. This inauthenticity is what holds us back, keeping us from sharing an opinion for fear of ridicule or rejection, social pain. This inauthentic self is overly agreeable, fearing the disruption of the unity of the group, and overly responsible, picking up balls that likely should have been dropped. An often-misunderstood aspect of the journey toward authentic selfhood is the necessary ridding of the false self. You can't be you *and* the persona you have been projecting to others for many years. It is your choice which you will be.

Many of us have been acting more extroverted than we are in an attempt to secure the favor of others, to belong, or even to get ahead. The price of this charade has been high. It has cost us the loss of the real us, the person who lives inside and longs for a visible and authentic expression in the world. Learning to feel all of the emotions we have been given is a key aspect of moving from this false self to the true one. Healthy rejection of cultural messaging, shame and the false self is the first step toward wholeness. But it doesn't end there.

HEALTHY ACCEPTANCE

Healthy acceptance is a powerful thing. It is not only our job to reject those things, people or ideas that continue to be detrimental to our healthy development, but to also replace what we reject with positive counterparts. Some people get stuck in rejection mode. They become more about what they aren't than what they are. We want to guard against that potential. Having pushed aside the negative messaging of the culture all around us, the shame that is a result of prolonged exposure to these toxins, and the false self we have developed to protect the real self from shame, we now need to accept the following three things:

We must first learn to *accept the culture* in which we are placed. This sounds contrary to what I said a few paragraphs ago. "I thought we were to reject the culture and its false messages," you might counter. And you would be right as a first step. When we first encounter the extrovert ideal, we are naturally and rightly angry. As introverts, it seems as if the deck is stacked against us. We move through understandable phases as we alternate between acceptance and rejection of cultural bias, understand its impact on us, and learn how to navigate these waters with wisdom and discernment. But, getting stuck will only hinder us. This is our reality, the context into which we have been placed. Accepting it does not mean condoning it.

Secondly, we learn to *accept ourselves* in a new and radical way. Who we are and how we are are not broken but merely a healthy counterpart to the extroverted way. Seeing this sets us free from the stigma that hinders us externally and internally. This is a simple concept yet profoundly difficult to do. It will likely involve the cultivation of new encouraging relationships. Self-acceptance and other-acceptance are connected, especially for more collectivistic people such as us. Understanding the biological differences between introversion and extroversion is key to this process.

Accepting ourselves will be evident in our new way of being. No longer will we apologize for who we are or how we approach situations. We will begin to understand that there is not one right way and that our natural approach is one of several needed for the overall good of the team. Who we are will begin to be something we can genuinely celebrate. We'll raise our hands as boldly and proudly as the extroverts do.

Thirdly, we need to learn to *accept our limitations*. Even though we have all been told over and over that we can do anything we set our mind to, we need to step back from that truism and think a little harder. On its face, it's simply not true. Don't try to be or keep up with extroverts. You'll wear out and you'll lose your true self seeking to become someone else. You're not them. You're you. Knowing your differences and limitations is good self-awareness.

This area of accepting limitations is directly related to the subject of self-care. Introverts are interdependently minded, other-oriented individuals. Because of this primary focus on others, they are greatly susceptible to self-neglect, burnout and other forms of self-damage. Self-care is critical for everyone, especially for introverts. The following is a list of practical aspects of self-care to which introverts especially need to pay attention:

- Watch your energy levels.

    o Are you getting enough sleep? Exercise? Down time? Quality time with significant others?

- Watch your schedule.

    o Are you overbooking yourself, especially with too many large groups?

    o Are you building in time for renewal?

- Be aware of over-stimulation.

    o Watch your caffeine intake.[2]

    o Watch your exposure to too many large groups and social events.

- Make sure you create space for yourself.

    o To think deeply about important things.

    o To read, study and investigate new ideas.

    o To have deeper, more meaningful conversations with significant others.

    o To make a difference in the world around you.

- Take time to be renewed.

  ○ As one author suggested, "Resist the temptation to see your urge for solitude as a 'liability,' and remember that alone time is the air introverts breathe. Time spent alone in a quiet environment will restore your energy and, more importantly, may give rise to a career-changing epiphany."[3]

If you do not accept your limitations, your body will kindly remind you. Understand that you will not be successful mimicking the patterns of an extrovert. You need to be you. Learning to be intentional about managing your limitations and caring for yourself well are critically important. These aspects of rejecting some things and accepting others are part of your identity reformation.

IDENTITY

At the core of our being is a central question, "Who am I?" Gershen Kaufman said it well:

The need for a secure, self-affirming identity that provides both continuity and meaning to the paths we travel lies at the core of each of us. Identity is a sense of self, of who one is and who one is not, and of where one belongs. It is a sense of inner centeredness and valuing.[4]

Kaufman went on to explain that shame is the antithesis. It intrudes into the question of identity and speaks lies at the core of who we are.

Our identity is something we should not have to apologize for. Who we are is not broken. Who we are is perfectly fine. Though we differ from extroverts around us, neither they nor we should be asked to be someone other than ourselves. We need to stop measuring ourselves with the wrong ruler. Instead, by assessing ourselves with the full picture of humanity in all of its glorious diversity, remarkably we discover that who we are is something to be celebrated. Neither extroversion nor introversion is better, just different. For both of us, the best is always to be ourselves.

Part of fully accepting our authentic identity is learning to be comfortable enough in our own skin to respond authentically to those around us. This chapter ends with a list of things we have thought often but, for fear of rejection, may not have said aloud. Get comfortable saying the following:

- Reading a book is doing something.

- I would prefer to sit this one out.

- That schedule is a bit too tight for me.

- I really don't enjoy large gatherings of people.

- Frankly, I'm too tired.

- Just because I didn't say anything does not mean I don't have any thoughts on the subject.

- I'd like to sleep on this decision.

- Can I get back to you in a few days?

- As an introvert . . .

- No, thank you.

- I don't do well in last minute situations. I need adequate time to prepare.

- I'm angry about what you said yesterday.

- It really makes me sad when . . .

- I'm afraid that . . .

Being comfortable with who we are frees us up from the trap of pretending to be someone we're not. Practicing simultaneous healthy rejection and acceptance is a great first step on our journey toward authentic leadership.

REFLECTION QUESTIONS

Accepting who you are is the first step to becoming the person and leader you were meant to be. Thinking about your own journey toward authenticity, consider the following questions.

1. What aspects of the *yang* culture around you do you need to reject?

2. How can you advance an understanding of introversion in your organization?

3. How can you reject stereotypes about introversion?

4. How can you reject shame? embrace creativity?

5. What aspects of the culture do you need to accept? How can you do this?

6. Can you truly accept yourself as you are? Why or why not?

7. What limitations do you have related to introversion? Have you accepted these realities that go along with being you?

8. Who are you?

Strengths & Weaknesses

"Our strength grows out of our weakness."

—Ralph Waldo Emerson

"I have amazing abilities to lead others, to build relationships, to understand complex problems, to plan and execute strategy," Kristi told me. She was an incredible woman who was very clear about who she was and what she brought to the organization she served. Kristi was one of the clearest introverts I interviewed.

Many of the individuals I interviewed listed common strengths centering on other-orientation. "I'm good at helping others, seeing what people need or want, reading their emotions, listening." They also saw strengths related to problem solving and focusing on quality results. "I'm good at organizing and expressing information and data (writing, spreadsheets, etc.) and finding the information for myself (research, problem solving)." They even reported strengths in presenting, noting that maximizing this strength relied on having "adequate time to prepare."

Kristi clearly understood her strengths and the value that she brought to the organization. She was also sure of her limitations. "I'm not good at working a room, butting into conversations, or acting and deciding with minimal information," she said. Common themes emerged around areas of difficulty. "I'm not good at telling people what I need and want [*assertiveness*]."

I heard similar clarity from other interviewees. One leader said, "I sometimes feel unheard in a group discussion, like either my voice must not be loud enough or my opinion is not sought." Another said, "I'm not so good at doing new things or doing things on the spot that I'm not comfortable/familiar/good at yet in front of people and sometimes asking for help [*change*]." One said, "I'm not good at charming people, influencing them [*charisma*]." Many of us struggle in particular in dealing with much more assertive and dominant people (extroverts). As one leader put it, "I struggle with having confidence in being a leader when the attacks come. Even though I don't quit, I have my moments of checking job boards when things are rough [*resilience*]."

Introversion is a more self-critical orientation and is prone toward an over focus on weaknesses, particularly lacking extroverted qualities in a *yang*-skewed culture of leadership. Should we simply focus more on our different, more introverted strengths? Yes, but there is an additional way to reframe this aspect of self-understanding. Could it be that some of these perceived weaknesses are actually strengths in disguise?

"Did you know that your natural pessimism is a strength?" I asked a group I was training. Long pause. Confused looks.

"It can't be. It drives everyone around me nuts," one woman replied.

"What about your tunnel vision? Can you see how that could actually be a strength?" I replied. In many areas, we may need to understand the relative nature of strengths and weaknesses, to actually redefine the parameters by which we determine the two.

THE COMPLETE LEADER

Many of us who are introverted watch some leaders in action and think to ourselves, "I wish I could be like that. He's so nimble on his feet and so confident. She seems to be free from so many of the things I struggle with." And then we are tempted to think, "He (or she) has it all together." Acting like those who have their act together can often be a failure to be authentic and real as a leader. Vulnerability is not a weakness; it's a strength. To admit that we don't have it all together is a freeing thing and a huge encouragement to those we lead. It creates higher levels of hope, trust, engagement and creativity for those around us.[1]

Part of our erroneous thinking is connected to yet another myth, the myth of the complete leader. Complete leaders are good at everything. They are charismatic, confident, firm, driven, results-oriented, safe, honest, thorough, detailed, careful, patient and the list goes on. When you find someone who is all of these things, run. Why? Because there is such a thing as "too good to be true." In reality, we're all incomplete leaders. This is how my friends and colleagues Ron Price and Randy Lisk have described the reality:

> What does it mean to be the complete leader? The truth is there is no such thing. Rather, a "complete leader" is always in the pursuit of completeness. In many ways, a more accurate term would be "incomplete leader" to describe someone who is always expanding his skills or knowledge. . . . The greatest leaders are always striving for more—always working to improve themselves and reach higher. . . . Becoming a complete leader is an aspirational vision. Nobody ever crosses the finish line.[2]

Not only are we always incomplete in the sense of not having arrived, we are also incomplete in the sense of being intrinsically designed to be interdependent. As we've seen, balance is only found with the combination of *yin* and *yang*. As it pertains to leadership, none of us has all that is needed to lead well. We each have differing gifts and strengths that the team or organization needs. This means that healthy and honest leaders are self-aware. They see their strengths and their weaknesses, but they also know who else in the circle of leadership is strong where they lack. In fact, Ron Price and Randy Lisk are a great example of *yang* and *yin* leaders. Ron is a high-I extrovert who is very engaging and charismatic, while Randy is a high-S and high-C introvert who is great with people in a slower-paced, comfortable way. The book they coauthored would not exist with either side of the equation lacking.

STRENGTHS & WEAKNESSES

This topic of strengths or weaknesses is often treated as a binary subject. In other words, I force myself to see that I have a strength or a weakness in a certain area, an either-or kind of question, rather than seeing I actually have a trait that can be both. As we've seen in relation to the *yin yang* idea throughout this book, oftentimes these discussions are better answered with both-and.

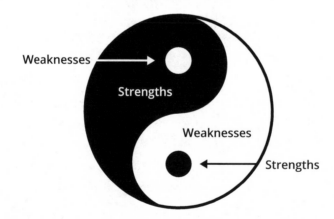

Figure 14, Strengths in weaknesses, weaknesses in strengths.

The *yin yang* symbol is a great metaphor for this topic of strengths (see figure 14). In reality, we normally have a drop of weakness in the midst of our strengths and a drop of strength in the midst of our weaknesses. Nothing is simple, but complex. As John Geier has pointed out, "A person's strength, when overused, or used inappropriately, becomes a weakness."[3] So, in the middle of our strength is a potential for weakness. It also works in the other direction. In the middle of our weaknesses, we can often identify strengths. Consider the following example to illustrate this principle.

One of the most obvious aspects of introversion is a natural pessimism, the ability to see the problems in plans or situations, the things that won't work. For us, the glass is perpetually half-empty. Though we try to practice optimism, it's not really our nature. This is normally framed as a weakness, especially by the overly optimistic *yang*-biased culture all around us. However, as we'll see, pessimism is one of the leading strengths found in most introverted leaders. Introverts possess wonderful and useful natural talents that can be viewed as strengths. To see our strengths in this new light, we need to reframe them, to see them differently than we usually do in our current cultural context.

STRENGTHS (& THEIR WEAKNESSES)

Ron and Randy have said it well: "Ever since childhood, most of us are taught to focus on our weaknesses."[4] Most families fall short on praise and encouragement and too frequently provide negative feedback. When we go to school, we soon learn that marks on our paper are usually bad things (especially if they are in red). For an introvert, with our natural propensity to see negativity much more clearly than encouragement, this sets us up on a futile mission, to get through school or life with as few red marks as possible. The goal becomes perfection and the rest is history. For many *yin* leaders, it is revolutionary to rethink this subject of strengths.

Focusing on our weaknesses comes naturally to us (we'll look at those shortly). What we introverts often need much more is a realistic look at our strengths. As you review the following *yin* strengths and see these traits in yourself, be aware that there are three major ways you need to respond to them. First, you need to *identify* them. Second, you need to *develop* them. And third, you need to *use* them. Here are typical strengths introverted leaders possess:

- *Pessimism.* As stated earlier, this gift is an asset to the team. Every group of people has the potential to blindly follow a misguided or problematic idea, plan or person. You have the ability to smell out problems by projecting negative future outcomes. Fear is a future-oriented emotion connected to our great ability to poke holes in ideas.

- *Tunnel vision.* Though the culture sees this as a problem, this kind of sustained focus is exactly what is needed to solve highly complex problems. Such issues require a healthy isolation and ability to focus with laser precision on a given situation.

- *Vulnerability.* By virtue of being on the *yin* side, you are most likely more vulnerable than some people. This feels like weakness from the inside, but from the outside, normally people see it as a strength.[5] In a recent article in *Harvard Business Review*, Emma Seppala explained the huge gains bosses experience by being vulnerable.[6] Her example was a South Indian leader of a technology company who created intense loyalty and high levels of engagement in those she supervised not by being strong, but by being vulnerable.

- *Emodiversity.* As we discussed in chapter nine, the ability to deeply experience the full spectrum of human emotions is a huge strength. Because you don't feel constrained to always be happy, you are able to connect with people at all different places on the emotional continuum.

- *Empathy.* This is directly related to *emodiversity.* Empathy is built on sadness, the ability to feel the sadness of others and to respond compassionately and empathetically. Empathy is not something you need when interacting with those who are prosperous or happy, but with those who are struggling and downcast. Your natural bent toward sadness makes you immediately qualified to develop deep empathy for others who suffer.

- *One-on-one interactions.* Introverts prefer deep conversations of care and concern with one individual over light, brief encounters with many people. This is a significant strength to leverage in a workplace that has more and more people looking for these deeper personal or mentoring relationships with leaders.

- *Calm, reasoned reflection.* We tend to think deeply, logically and long before we speak. This strength is in contrast to much of the hype or overenthusiastic emotional appeals that often prevail in the workplace.

- *More conventional strengths.* In addition to these ironic strengths, you also likely have some of the following normally discussed strengths as well:

  o *Listening.* Introverts excel at listening. We tend to contribute fewer words to the conversation. We are often great natural listeners and excellent at asking questions, drawing content out of those we are seeking to serve.

  o *Understanding others.* Because a *yin* orientation tends to be other-centered and interdependent-focused, we tend to be good at understanding others, getting where they are coming from. This skill is somewhat related to the skills of empathy and listening.

- *Creativity.* Albert Einstein famously said, "We cannot solve our problems with the same thinking we used to create them."[7] There is a significant overlap between highly creative people and introversion. Oftentimes, creativity requires many hours of working alone, thinking deeply. Removing the shame that constricts creativity is a critical task for innovative introverts.

- *Wisdom and prudence.* If you read the Hebrew wisdom literature (Psalms and Proverbs), you'll clearly see the connection between the wise person and traits we would today identify with introversion. Introverts tend to go carefully, thoughtfully and cautiously, not taking any unnecessary risks in the process. This is the definition of wisdom or an old word we don't use much in our happiness culture, prudence.

- *Thinking and analyzing.* I love Susan Cain's comment on this. She said, "There's a word for 'people who are in their heads too much': thinkers."[8] We are tailor-made for this kind of work.

- *Planning and organization.* Introverts tend to be naturals at planning, organization and preparation. They are capable of the focus required to develop extremely well-thought-out plans.

- *Problem solving.* We are natural problem solvers whose brains continue to work, even subconsciously, until the problem under consideration is solved.[9] We tend to have the discipline to stay focused and push for answers, along with a greater capacity for "sustained and concentrated work."[10]

- *Educational attainment.* Levels of education often correlate to success as a leader. Though education is not the only indicator, it is a significant one. Introversion is consistently connected to higher levels of educational achievement.[11]

o *Written communication.* Though many introverted leaders would report a perceived deficiency in oral communication (in front of larger groups), most introverts excel when it comes to writing. This is likely a sweet spot you need to continue to leverage and exploit.

o *Public speaking.* You may be surprised to see this in the strengths list. Did you know that fear of public speaking is one of the largest fears for everyone (extroverts and introverts both)? Most people fear public speaking at some level. Many introverts are outstanding public speakers (e.g., Susan Cain, Malcolm Gladwell, Barack Obama). In fact, speaker and executive coach Jennifer Kahnweiler suggested that over fifty percent of the people who earn a living by speaking are introverts.[12] Malcolm Gladwell, who speaks regularly, brilliantly noted, "Speaking is not an act of extroversion. It has nothing to do with extroversion. It's a performance, and many performers are hugely introverted."[13] The key for introverts and speaking is to be well prepared. Practice, practice, practice. You can also do power posing before you speak.[14] This is a term coined by Amy Cuddy to describe the power pose—hands on hips, chest out like Superman—for two minutes just prior to "going on stage," whether it's an actual stage or just a situation in which you're feeling insecure. You can do a power pose in the bathroom stall, the elevator or another private space. Her theory suggests that the power pose actually increases confidence and one's sense of power.

WEAKNESSES (& THEIR STRENGTHS)

While I generally agree that we should spend the majority of our energy developing our natural strengths, I disagree with those who are so strength-focused that weaknesses are ignored.[15] I suspect that some of this tendency is another aspect of the strange obsession our culture has with positivity. We all have them, the "w" word. To pretend we don't or to not talk about them actually robs us of the trust that comes ironically from honesty and vulnerability with each other. Sometimes we soften our language and call them challenges or obstacles, but I think it's healthiest to call them weaknesses, things we're not as good at.

It seems as if we have three major options as it relates to typical *yin* leader weaknesses. We can *develop* them. We can *neutralize* them. We can *work around* them. I suggest only developing a weakness that is a critical strength needed in your particular role or position. If not, think about the other two options. You need to decide if this weakness is something you can work around, perhaps partnering with others on your team who have this strength, or something you need to neutralize, making it more of a non-issue. People may still see it as one of your lesser strengths, but it won't stick out and call as much attention to itself. Here are some of the most common weaknesses with brief strategies to neutralize each:

- *Resilience and flexibility.* Introverts do not normally bounce back quickly from setbacks and difficult situations. As we reviewed in chapter six, the release of adrenaline and dopamine in a scary situation does not feel good to introverts as it does to many extroverts. We have a little longer cycle. Flexibility is similar to resilience. How well do you adjust to change? Do you like surprises? As introverts, we don't like change, especially not rapid and unexpected change in our environment.

Suggestions to neutralize: Give yourself permission not to react in the moment. When surprises happen, get in the habit of creating space and room to process the unexpected changes. When you experience adversity and disappointment, process your true feelings with others who are safe for you.

- *Decisiveness.* This is more of a *yang* (high D) strength and a *yin* (high S or C) weakness. Do you ever struggle with making decisions in a timely way? Why? I suspect that you struggle with timeliness due to your inner desire for perfection.

  Suggestions to neutralize: Put yourself on a deadline that connects with the bigger picture. Seek the counsel of others you respect and gather data within that window of time. If you need to make a decision, make the best one you can with the data you have gathered, knowing that perfection is unrealistic.

- *Brainstorming.* Which do you prefer, a brainstorming session or a root canal? I suspect a root canal. As we saw in chapter six, our brains take the longer path through Broca's area and the frontal cortex and work on complex problems during sleep, neither of which fits well with the brainstorming mode.

  Suggestions to neutralize: Suggest to your team that you use a hybrid process for brainstorming. There can still be an in-person component, but providing, for example, a good agenda two days prior with the topics identified also gives introverts time to begin processing the issues. There should also be a way to provide input after the meeting, when introverts' best ideas come to them (often in their sleep).[16] I sometimes call this leaving a back door open for input.

- *Networking.* Most introverts don't particularly like "working the room," at a networking event. The reality, however, is that introverts are good at building deeper relationships, nurturing and providing customer service. All of these can be leveraged to build effective, rather than overly large, networks. Bigger may not be better, just bigger.

  Suggestions to neutralize: Leverage your natural relational skills to build networking relationships with key people one person at a time. Use social media to your advantage, and don't worry as much about how many followers you have. Redefine how you think about networking, perhaps by following the example of Reid Hoffman, the cofounder of LinkedIn, who calls himself a "six-person-or-less extrovert," optimizing himself "for less than six people, preferably one-on-one."[17]

- *Sales.* When you hear the word "sales," what do you feel? Many introverts shudder to think of the self-promotion or networking often connected to the Western stereotype of sales. The good news, however, is that the myth that extroverts make the best salespeople is overblown.[18] The evidence for the correlation between extroversion and sales performance is nil.[19] In fact, ambiverts, in the middle of the temperamental spectrum, may have an advantage in relating to all points along the continuum and may be accordingly best suited for sales.[20] In this way, what is seen as a weakness in some non-extroverts may actually be a misunderstood strength.

  Suggestions to neutralize: Use your deep relationships with others to create a network of sales leads, based not on marketing or hype but on the substance of your past work. Partner with extroverts to leverage their outgoing nature and lead generation and together work to not only close the deal but to deliver extraordinary service, leading to referrals and additional business.

- *Self-promotion.* This is an oxymoron to *yin* people. We are not about "me" but "we." Self-promotion doesn't normally come naturally to introverts. We tend to avoid the limelight and prefer to see ourselves as part of the group. We usually see ourselves and our faults so clearly that promoting ourselves can become awkward or difficult. *Suggestions to neutralize*: According to the introverted expert and author Nancy Ancowitz, we should learn the art of self-promotion that is neither schmoozing nor cheerleading.[21] Self-promotion for introverts is entirely different. We need to leverage our abilities in writing, researching and listening to our promotional advantage by creating good written or other content that promotes our expertise. Our expertise, coming from our careful, thoughtful research can help promote a higher cause or purpose. In this way, we will feel more comfortable promoting a cause or a purpose rather than simply ourselves.

- *Multitasking.* How many "balls" can you juggle at one time? There is limited research regarding introversion and multitasking. However, a 2001 study by Lieberman and Rosenthal showed some evidence for a reduction in multitasking ability connected to introversion.[22] It seems logical that introverts, with a longer neural path and deeper focus of concentration, would be more distracted by additional tasks and have a harder time rapidly switching between them. I have noticed that I do not do well with too many things to juggle at once. I do far better with deeper sustained focus on one thing at a time.

Suggestions to neutralize: You are the one who determines the number and spacing of the appointments or tasks you agree to. Knowing about your nature, you can intentionally establish your calendar of projects, tasks and interactions in a way that maximizes your need to focus deeply on one thing. Work to reduce the constant interruptions that distract you from your best results.

- *Conflict management.* When you hear the "c" word, what is your emotional response? Many introverts have a natural aversion to conflict. In fact, most people do.[23] However, you still need to become skilled at resolving and managing conflict. In many ways, the patient, logical, less emotionally volatile nature of a high-S introvert and the factual, reasonable approach of a high-C introvert are helpful, behavioral traits when working in highly charged and highly emotional conflict situations.

  Suggestions to neutralize: Avoid your natural tendency to avoid conflict and confront it earlier and more decisively.[24] Use your logical and factual tendencies to gather objective data related to the conflict situation. Utilize your ability to stay calm to keep the focus on specific behaviors and actions rather than looking for character flaws in individuals.

DEVELOPING COMPETENCE

There is a fundamental difference between a natural talent and a developed competence. Any of our current strengths can be further reinforced and developed. A strength developed becomes a competency. Weaknesses that are critical areas of skill for a position can also be developed. Whether building on natural talent or not, there is no shortcut to competency development. Mastering a skill requires the use of the three Ps: practice, practice, practice.

I work with Price Associates, an organization that helps leaders grow and impact their worlds. One of the ways we help leaders grow is through developing identified workplace competencies that will take their leadership to the next level. We currently measure twenty-five workplace leadership competencies.[25] To see your current level of development around these competencies, visit The Complete Leader site (www.thecompleteleader.org) and take a free twelve-question sample assessment.

The first step toward competency development is gaining an accurate perception of a leader's current level of development as a starting point. We can get a clear picture of our current levels through a combination of self-assessment and 360-degree feedback, feedback from others above, around or below us in the organization. Woven into the coaching, team development or leadership development processes I utilize with clients are specific and relevant competencies related to superior performance in any position.

For introverted leaders, one of the biggest challenges lies in reframing perceived weaknesses as strengths and allowing ourselves to reject culturally imposed standards of leadership. This is a constant putting off of the cultural stereotypes and putting on of an alternate, more *yin*-friendly construct of strengths.

REFLECTION QUESTIONS

Think about both your strengths and weaknesses as you consider the following questions.

1. What are you great at? What would your organization miss the most if you were gone?

2. How are you leveraging those strengths for the sake of the organization?

3. Have you always seen your strengths as "strengths"?

4. What perceived weaknesses do you have that might actually be strengths?

5. What are your areas of weakness that are not critical to your performance? What can you stop focusing on trying to improve?

6. What is the one thing at the top of your list for improvement?

13

Leaders & Balance

"We know that every successful organization has, at its heart, a cadre of co-leaders—key players who do the work, even if they receive little of the glory."

—David Heenan & Warren Bennis

In chapter four, you read the story of the Continental Congress that met in 1776 to discuss the problems related to King George's leadership. They met that summer to create a formal document explaining the rationale for the revolution they had undertaken. The Congress was well aware of the preliminary documents that John Adams had previously prepared connected to the May 10th Resolution of Independence. Some had even thought of that day as the real Independence Day. Adams, therefore, was the logical choice to lead the development of the final document.

Earlier, on June 11, the Congress had selected a committee of five to finish the writing task in preparation for the July meeting. Forty-year-old attorney John Adams; seventy-year-old inventor, publisher, and statesman Ben Franklin; thirty-three-year-old attorney Thomas Jefferson; and two others, Roger Sherman and Roger Livingston, were selected.

Adams surprisingly deferred to the younger Jefferson to prepare the first draft. Jefferson completed his first version cautiously, knowing he was the least experienced of the group. Shortly after his text began, it declared the following about human rights:

> We hold these truths to be sacred and undeniable; that all men are created equal & independent, that from that equal creation they derive in rights inherent & inalienable, among which are the preservation of life, liberty, and the pursuit of happiness.[1]

Jefferson, the hesitant author of the declaration, had penned one of the most influential statements in human history. That phrase continues to inform societies and the cause of equality. It also informs our current struggle as introverts.

The committee of five made their revisions and amendments. The revised document was finally approved by the entire assembly, receiving a total of fifty-six signatures. Remarkably, led by Jefferson and the committee, this gathering of only white, landowning men had produced one of the clearest statements on human rights in human history.[2] They likely had no idea how the ideals they advocated would one day be used to justify the abolition of slavery, the civil rights movement, women's suffrage and other occasions of inequality crying out for a clear application of these principles.

Who would be first to sign this dangerous and treasonous document? To sign would be a death sentence. A young merchant by the name of John Hancock, the president of the Continental Congress and one of the Sons of Liberty, stepped forward and largely, proudly and famously went first. He was the only one to sign the document that day. Other signatories followed between August 2 and November 4. The signed document was distributed throughout the colonies and to King George across the Atlantic.

Great leadership relies on an interworking between leaders along the entire continuum from *yin* (introversion) to *yang* (extroversion). The Congress achieved what it did because it was a cooperative effort between both introverted and extroverted leaders. Jefferson and Adams were both clear introverts. They exercised their superior gifts of written communication and conceptual thinking to give shape on paper to the ideals of the new nation.

Franklin and Hancock were clear extroverts. Franklin, who had given many inspiring speeches to the Second Continental Congress on the subject of liberty and freedom from British oppression, played a key role on the committee and in support of Jefferson. Franklin would also have the broadest influence related to the American cause both in the colonies and across the ocean. Hancock exercised leadership in the moment by being the first to courageously step forward and take the risk of signing his own death sentence.

Great leadership exists at the point where these two necessary traits find balance (*he*). We see this partnership in all great civilizations throughout history. As psychologist Elaine Aron pointed out:

> The most long-lasting, happy Indo-European cultures have always used two classes to govern themselves—the warrior-kings [*yang*] balanced by their royal or priestly advisors [*yin*] . . . . [T]o perform our [*yin*] role well, we have to feel very good about ourselves. We have to ignore all the messages from the warriors [*yang*] that we are not as good as they are. The warriors have their bold style, which has its value. But we, too, have *our* style and our own important contribution to make. (italics added)[3]

Notably absent from the process was the idea that either extroverted or introverted leaders are better. Instead of settling for solitary leadership, the colonists opted for balanced leadership as represented by the committee and the broader Continental Congress.

WHO MAKES THE BEST PIZZA?

In an interesting 2010 study, a team of researchers led by Adam Grant of the Wharton School of the University of Pennsylvania set out to understand a nagging question in the leadership world. Who makes the best leaders?

Adam Grant and I both identify as social introverts. A social introvert is someone who is slower-paced, inward-oriented, and stimulation-averse, who loves people in usually smaller doses, is not shy and enjoys talking long and deeply with them. Though Grant conceded that the literature is extremely biased in favor of extroversion as a prerequisite trait for leadership, he and the research team wanted to test leadership effectiveness as it relates to different kinds of followers. The setting of their study was a group of pizza franchises.[4]

What they found was encouraging. Who makes the best leaders? It depends. For those workers who are highly self-motivated and proactive, introverts were the most effective leaders. For those workers who were lacking in self-motivation and more passive, extroverts created a healthier bottom line. Leadership is not a one-size-fits-all concept. The diverse nature of groups and organizations suggests that the best leadership solution is found in the combination of divergent leadership styles working together.

Another study in the Australian military found that superior leadership was not connected to higher levels of extroversion, but instead to lower levels of extroversion, a.k.a. introversion, and higher levels of conscientiousness, a trait that in many ways connects to the description of high-C introversion in the DISC model.[5] There is ample evidence of the value and need for introverted leaders to complement extroverted ones.[6]

This is huge news in light of the demographic trends related to the takeover of the millennials. In the last few years, a demographic trend has begun that will continue indefinitely. As boomers leave the workforce in droves and busters' (Gen X) participation remains relatively flat, the millennials (Gen Y) will continue to occupy an expanding proportion of the workforce and leadership in American organizations.[7] For the most part, contrary to much popular mythology, these millennials tend to be more proactive in the workplace, just the types of team members that *yin* leaders are well suited to lead.

YIN LEADERS

Yin leaders, according to a recent article by Jennifer Kahnweiler, are uniquely suited to lead in the emerging millennial culture. She specifically noted four *yin* strengths we observed in the last chapter that connect with the identified needs of millennials at work: one-on-one interactions, listening and asking great questions, preparation and careful planning, and calm and reasoned reflection.[8] Millennials are looking for the kinds of leaders we'll explore in depth shortly: planned, analytical, team-oriented and wise.[9] They want leaders focused not just on the bottom line but on making the world a better place.

It comes as a surprise to many that some of the most successful entrepreneurs in our culture are actually *yin* leaders. I have used the term *intropreneur* to describe this new breed of intensely successful leader and innovator that is clearly on the introverted side of the equation. Current intropreneurs include Warren Buffett (one of the wealthiest men in the world), Bill Gates (the founder of Microsoft), Mark Zuckerberg (the founder of Facebook), Tony Hsieh (the founder of Zappos), Larry Page (the cofounder of Google), and Reid Hoffman (the cofounder of LinkedIn).

For this reason, some have suggested that "self-aware 'innies,' when they maximize their talents, can flourish in entrepreneurship and other fields once thought to be only the province of 'outies.'"[10] This is consistent with the findings of psychologist Hans Eysenck, who many years ago found that successful business people were, on the whole, stable (non-neurotic) introverts who were able to leverage their self-sufficient, hardworking attitudes and introspective, analytical style of leadership.[11] These *yin* leaders operate from a mixture of slow-paced, safe, cautious, team-related focus and quality-driven, project-focused, analytical, creative and detail-oriented focus. Four kinds of leaders can be identified on the *yin* side:

Planned Leaders pay attention to the details of the plan and make sure the team gets everything done that it needs to while maintaining the highest levels of quality. They see the trees individually and not just the forest. Their close-up view often complements the *yang* leaders' view from thirty-five thousand feet.

Analytical Leaders use deep-thinking skills to solve complex problems for the sake of the team. They look deeply into objective facts, study situations and leverage a natural creativity to arrive at sound decisions that will benefit the group.

Team Leaders are masterful in connecting the team together, creating safety, security and belonging. They stay focused on team cohesion and the development of organizational culture. They are about "us."

Wise Leaders take measured risks after carefully weighing pros and cons and thinking deeply and logically about options. They are not impulsive or reactionary. Instead, having a natural aversion to overemotional hype that sometimes leads to bad decisions, the wise leader is very intentional and stays focused on making good, rational decisions.

Who are these *yin* leaders? History has given examples of the good, the bad and the ugly. Here is a sampling of introverted *yin* leaders from history:

For Good	For Ill
• Moses	• Adolf Hitler
• Socrates	• Vladimir Putin
• Gandhi	• Francisco Franco
• Soren Kierkegaard	• Osama bin Laden
• Charles Darwin	• Mohamed Atta
• Abraham Lincoln	• Ayatollah Khomeini
• Mother Teresa	• Chiang Kai-shek
• George Washington	• Heinrich Himmler
• Joe DiMaggio	• Vladimir Lenin
• Martin Luther	• David Koresh

Table 2. Good and bad introverted leaders

YANG LEADERS

We also, however, need *yang* leaders. When the Titanic runs into the iceberg, we need an extrovert in charge, organizing the process of getting everyone into the lifeboats. If an introverted leader is at the helm when we hit the iceberg, we might waste time conducting a research study on the pros on cons of different lifeboat seating configurations. We also need more *yang*-oriented leaders to provide vision and inspiration for the team and to keep us hopeful and optimistic about the future. *Yang* leaders tend to have a combination of four different leadership traits:

Crisis Leaders take charge when time is of the essence. They don't waste time overanalyzing the situation, but respond automatically or instinctually. These are typically great leaders in the military, law enforcement, and other institutions and organizations that require regular and ongoing crisis management.

Results Leaders keep us focused and on task. They are driven to see results reflected in the bottom line. Investors love these kinds of leaders. They tend to be driven and motivated to see projects realized, profits maintained and growth achieved.

Visionary Leaders inspire us and help us dream larger dreams. They help us see the bigger picture, often emphasizing the forest instead of the trees. They tend to cast a picture of the future that becomes a shared vision, driving team goals and objectives.

Hopeful Leaders keep us motivated when the going gets tough. They inspire hope for better days ahead and give us the courage to keep moving forward until those days become reality. They leverage optimism to keep hope, a critical commodity for the team, from diminishing in the midst of adversity or challenge.

History also gives us examples of both good and bad *yang* leaders:

For Good	For Ill
• Martin Luther King, Jr.	• Mao Tse-tung
• Ronald Reagan	• Yasser Arafat
• Margaret Thatcher	• Jim Jones
• Bill Clinton	• Joseph Goebbels
• Sigmund Freud	• Joseph Stalin
• John F. Kennedy	• Benito Mussolini
• Winston Churchill	• Idi Amin
• Pope Francis	• Niccolo Machiavelli

Table 3. Good and bad extroverted leaders

In the best world, *yin* and *yang* leaders work synergistically in a mutually valuing and beneficial relationship with each other that best serves the entire team.

COMPLEMENTARY LEADERSHIP

We began this journey with an understanding of the *yin* and *yang* of life and the need for balance (*he*). Nowhere is this truer than in the realm of leadership in any organization or group. Some have applied this principle literally, creating coequal CEOs. Others have taken a less literal approach but still maintain the principle that "co-leadership should permeate every organization at every level."[12]

We've seen the Wozniak-Jobs partnership and should notice that this kind of pairing of *yin* and *yang* is common in successful organizations of all kinds. Other famous examples include Eleanor and Franklin Roosevelt in the White House, Mark Zuckerberg and Sheryl Sandberg at Facebook, Larry Page and Sergey Brin at Google, and Bill Gates and Steve Ballmer at Microsoft. None of these leaders can take credit for company success without acknowledging the other.

Great leaders (and terrible ones) emerge from all parts of the introvert-extrovert spectrum. This is consistent with the thoughts of one of the greatest leadership and management minds of the past century, Peter Drucker. In his 1992 book, *Managing for the Future*, he famously bemoaned the misguidedness of the conversation about leadership.[13] He clearly saw that leadership didn't depend on charisma, nor any "personality traits" or "qualities," but on hard work.

For Drucker, hard work consisted of three things. First, the leader's work is to clearly establish *vision*, goals and purpose for the organization, a vision sufficiently large to sustain team motivation over the long haul. Second, Drucker saw leadership as needing to be about *responsibility* rather than privilege. Good leaders see themselves as the one ultimately responsible for the state of affairs in the organization. Last, Drucker saw *trust* as the indispensable commodity on which leadership is built. So, whatever one's temperament or personality style, Drucker would say leadership is about hard work: staying clear, being responsible and building trust.

All types of leaders can accomplish these three as they work alongside dissimilar yet complementary leaders around the table. Figure 15 shows the balance of the eight types of leaders we need.

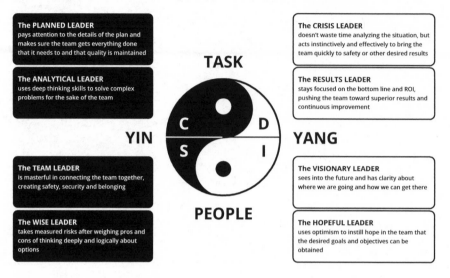

The PLANNED LEADER pays attention to the details of the plan and makes sure the team gets everything done that it needs to and that quality is maintained

The ANALYTICAL LEADER uses deep thinking skills to solve complex problems for the sake of the team

TASK

The CRISIS LEADER doesn't waste time analyzing the situation, but acts instinctively and effectively to bring the team quickly to safety or other desired results

The RESULTS LEADER stays focused on the bottom line and ROI, pushing the team toward superior results and continuous improvement

YIN C D **YANG** S I

The TEAM LEADER is masterful in connecting the team together, creating safety, security and belonging

The VISIONARY LEADER sees into the future and has clarity about where we are going and how we can get there

PEOPLE

The WISE LEADER takes measured risks after weighing pros and cons of thinking deeply and logically about options

The HOPEFUL LEADER uses optimism to instill hope in the team that the desired goals and objectives can be obtained

Figure 15. The eight types of leaders.

The world around us is often the world of "or." We compare two contrasting things or even individuals and seek to understand which is best. Instead, the balance (*he*) we need, as exemplified in the world all around us, consists in a complementary relationship between differing principles or people. The two different things held together comprise one whole.

Often, we may merely tolerate or even be intolerant of different people on our leadership teams. In the worst of cases, we may even devalue them, treating them as unworthy of dignity and respect. Tolerance, what so many preach in our world, is not enough, though. To tolerate different people is to put up with them, to allow them to be, but not to take the time and emotional energy to deeply know and value them. Tolerance is a very low standard and far below the ideal that *he* suggests. In actuality, the healthiest of leaders, who together lead the healthiest of organizations, deeply value fellow leaders with differing talents, temperaments and skills.

Valuing goes beyond tolerating and sees the genuine good in the differences. We are always better leading together than in isolation. Just as the Continental Congress discovered, *yin* and *yang* working together can produce revolutionary results. That being said, one thing remains, the ability to step forward as our authentic selves in the leadership roles that suit us uniquely and, as a part of the leadership team, lead. Authenticity is directly connected to our ability to value ourselves and others.

REFLECTION QUESTIONS

The most effective leadership teams I've worked with not only have balance but also value each other as the uniquely differing leaders they are. Think about your own experiences as you consider the following questions.

1. Why did it take both *yin* and *yang* leaders to create and sign the Declaration of Independence? Why is this significant?

2. Why do you think the idea that extroverts make better leaders continues in our society?

3. How much do you know about the millennials in the workforce? How can you leverage your introverted strengths to meet their needs?

4. Which of the eight leaders are you (you may be more than one)? The *yin* leader types are planned, analytical, team and wise. The *yang* leader types are crisis, results, visionary and hopeful.

5. Which kinds of leaders on the opposite side (*yang*) are the most difficult for you to collaborate with? Why? What can you do to improve collaboration with them?

6. Are you convinced of the need for balanced collaborative leadership?

7. Do you deeply and genuinely value extroverted leaders? introverted leaders? ambiverted leaders? How do you demonstrate that you value them?

14

Authenticity & Leadership

"The most important kind of freedom is to be what you really are. You trade in your reality for a role. You trade in your sense for an act. You give up your ability to feel, and in exchange, put on a mask. There can't be any large-scale revolution until there's a personal revolution, on an individual level. It's got to happen inside first."

—Jim Morrison

It seems fitting in this last chapter to tell a piece of my own journey. Because extroversion was valued in my family growing up, I either resisted awareness or was oblivious of my more introverted nature. Especially from college forward into early adult life in the workplace, I lived my life looking like an extrovert. I never took a personality test of any kind until I was in my late thirties. When I did take the first one as a counseling student, I was relieved to have been found just barely on the extroverted side of the line, because this seemed to be the right answer.

As I moved into middle age, I found good success in the field of architecture and led the firm I had started into some very prosperous years. I was the leader of the firm, the leader of its culture, development and finances. My role included taking the lead in business development and client relations. I believe my partners and clients would tell you I was a good leader.

I was therefore surprised that in subsequent years, after leaving architecture to pursue another career, my ability to lead would be questioned, more than once, on the basis of my introverted nature. It was the same introverted nature that caused me to look outside of architecture for a place to more directly serve and help others. Not yet fully understanding my own temperament, I was surprised to be perceived as overly analytical, overly fearful, and overly concerned with things being right and ethical. I was criticized for these *yin* traits and told I wasn't "leadership material." Extroverts criticized me for not being "engaging enough, funny enough, happy enough." It was very confusing and painful to me.

The extrovert ideal has been imposed on me several times. Each time I have been measured with the wrong ruler, I have been found wanting in risk tolerance, enthusiasm about change, optimism and other extroverted traits. More than once, I have been accused of "being depressed." It is a strange thing to have an alleged mental diagnosis be used against you as a weapon. I have been deeply impacted by this cultural bias that was ill fitting for me. I have experienced sadness as a result of this mistreatment and the connected losses, but it is clearly normal sadness with cause. I can see exactly where it comes from.

As I began to understand the principles I describe throughout this book, I began to move through the stages of cultural identity noted in the introduction: conformity, dissonance, resistance, introspection, articulation and awareness. I moved from not knowing I was an introvert, to knowing it and feeling marginalized, to feeling mad about being marginalized, to moving through anger toward healthy grief and sadness over the losses incurred in the process. Finally, I began to come to a more mature understanding of introverts and extroverts existing in a complementary relationship of mutual understanding, valuing and cooperation. This has been a process and it remains incomplete. I haven't arrived. But I'm on the journey now.

The most important aspect of this movement has been the development of an increasingly unapologetic acceptance of self. Like Doug Conant, the former CEO of Campbell Soup Company, I have found that "declaring my introversion," coming out of the closet if you will, has been "a very freeing exercise—more preferred than going through painful contortions in attempting to adapt to other people's styles."[1]

Though old habits die hard, I no longer apologize (as often) for being who I am or for seeing life or accomplishing goals as it comes naturally to me. This is a good sign pointing to an ever-emerging sense of authenticity in my approach to life and leadership. Being congruent, the internal reality matching the external reality, has become my ultimate end and personal goal in life. It is only when we are our true selves, the ones we were made to be, that we can begin to make our uniquely authentic mark on the world and fulfill our highest purpose.

AUTHENTICITY

Before you or I can be a leader, we need to be a person, a real person. Not a hero, or the mighty likeable fellow, or superhuman like many of the older models of leadership contend.[2] Real people experience the full span of human emotions and experiences. They exhibit a range of behavioral styles. They're motivated by different things and approach life from distinct angles. We are all unique, wonderfully so. Diversity is a beautiful thing and to be fully embraced. Learning to be your authentic self, especially as an introvert in an extroverted, happiness-obsessed, driven world, is a challenge worth pursuing.

Many things worth doing are difficult. As Bill George, a former CEO and Harvard professor, wrote,

> Becoming an authentic leader is not easy. First you have to understand yourself, because the hardest person you will ever have to lead is yourself. Once you have an understanding of your authentic self, you will find that leading others is much easier.[3]

For all leaders, but even more importantly for introverted leaders, this first step of self-understanding is critical.

The process of becoming your true self lies at the foundation of your leadership. It all begins and ends with authenticity. Authenticity, though, is an often misunderstood commodity.

Mike Robbins, the author of *Be Yourself, Everybody Else Is Taken: Transform Your Life with the Power of Authenticity*, gave a recent TED Talk that helped me to better articulate what authenticity is.[4] Robbins explained that authenticity is part of a continuum. It is distinguished from phoniness, which should come as no surprise. But what he said next surprised me and resonated deeply. He described the continuum as shown in figure 16:

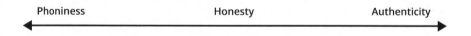

| Phoniness | Honesty | Authenticity |

Figure 16. Mike Robbins' continuum of authenticity.

Robbins explained that authenticity is beyond honesty. Being honest is easier. We can be honest and yet terribly cruel and invalidating toward others. Being authentic is more personal. It involves being real in a way that is vulnerable, that "liberates us and deeply touches those around us." As I listened to Robbins, I heard echoes of Brené Brown's descriptions of vulnerability. I knew then that these were closely related concepts. To be real, to be vulnerable, to be authentic is to let our true selves be seen and known, to no longer hide as shame wants us to, but to dare greatly, to be courageous.[5] This is the kind of authenticity introverted leaders need to pursue.

Robbins talked about this kind of authenticity as lowering the water level and allowing more of the iceberg underneath to be seen. In the past, many of us have not lowered the water level but raised it, hiding even more of ourselves from the gaze of others who have invalidated us. In a community of love, belonging and safety, we can begin to be healed from the effects of toxic shame and become the people we were made to be. This is the kind of authenticity that serves as the apex of the *yin* leader's movement toward becoming whole.

LEADING

Being your true self is the first half. Leading others is the second. According to an ancient Afghan proverb, "If you think you're leading and no one's following, you may discover that you're just out for a walk." As Peter Drucker said, a simple definition of leadership is "having followers."[6] Is it that simple? Is leadership just about getting people to follow you? Or is it about something much greater? Ron Price has suggested that leadership is about "influencing others."[7] These are both adequate definitions of the work of leadership. However we describe it, it is most often conceived of as a special class to which some belong and to which others only aspire. The few, the proud are leaders. The rest?

We are in the midst of a paradigm shift as it pertains to leadership. The old concept was built on the fundamental idea that leaders were special, larger than life, even heroic people. As Reid Hoffman pointed out, "the self-made man makes a good story."[8] This "great man" (sorry, ladies) myth is still largely a part of our collective cultural subconscious. The "great man" has the "right stuff," usually relating to inborn traits of temperament or personality.

This leadership ideal has perhaps run its course. As Hoffman suggested, these "tidy narratives tend to oversimplify reality."[9] We have begun to question the simple stories of greatness. This questioning has been encouraged as a result of an increasing crisis of trust in these so-called great men. Author Donovan Campbell described the problem we are facing:

> America suffers from a leadership crisis. . . . [I]nstitutions that define our views of ourselves and of our country, among them business and government, have lost substantial credibility. These leaders are largely viewed as greedy, selfish, hypocritical, criminal, shortsighted, incompetent, or all of the above. The widespread destruction of trust has left a leadership vacuum that is slowly becoming filled with despair. . . . We have lost faith in our leaders, and when faith leaves, hope soon follows. . . . America has lost faith in its leaders precisely because those leaders have done exactly what the books have said to do.[10]

Many of these great men have proven to be less than inspiring to those they dominate. We can only hope we are on the verge of a revolution in terms of the paradigm of leadership in the workplace. Maybe, as author Peter Shankman suggested, nice companies and collaborative leaders will actually finish first.[11]

An alternative model of leadership was offered by the social psychologists S. Alexander Haslam, Stephen Reicher and Michael Platow.[12] It is a model based on a more democratic understanding of leadership as a symbiotic relationship between leaders and followers. Based on social identity theory, the leader and the followers both share a common group identity. Leaders lead as one of *us*, doing it for *us*, helping to clarify *our* values, and together with *us* make *our* values come to realization. These new leaders do not lead from a hierarchal place of superiority but from among the tribe.[13] As Haslam et al. described, these new leaders' skills are summarized in the three Rs:

- *Reflecting.* Leaders are good at listening to the values, thoughts and dreams of those they lead. They watch, observe, interact with and learn the unique values and motivations of the group of which they are a part.

- *Representing.* They represent the shared vision, the why of the group, not merely their own individualistic dream. They recognize it's not about them but about the team. All of their policies, projects or proposals reflect the group's representative and collective ideals.

- *Realizing.* Understanding the shared vision of the group and deeply representing its values, leaders work to help the team bring this envisioned world to reality. This is the fulfillment of a shared why, the highest purpose.

This new leadership paradigm is very different. It leaves room for leaders at all levels of the organization and of all types and attributes. What is most important is the connection of the leader, of whatever type, to the group.

All three of these factors—a new leadership paradigm, a resurgence of more interdependently minded *yin* culture, and robustly ideological millennial values—may well be converging, uniquely setting up introverted leaders for such a time as this. This is your leadership opportunity. By being the authentic person you are, one that happens to naturally embody interdependently oriented traits, you are well positioned to step up and lead as part of a healthy and balanced leadership team.

It's not about removing extroverts from leadership, but about joining them with an equally valuable place at the table. It's about moving into a new vision of shared leadership that is reflective of the balance needed in all of life. Our culture has been imbalanced for too long. This is your opportunity to right the ship and step courageously forward as the authentic leader you are.

The time is now to recover from being devalued, marginalized or even ostracized. Working back through the pain, you are moving into a new day of clarity about who you are and your readiness for the task at hand. You are not broken. There is nothing wrong with you. Who you are is wonderful. Shame is a liar.

The world needs you in order to move toward a greater sense of wholeness. What remains is the courage to step forward. Will you answer the call?

REFLECTION QUESTIONS

Understanding that authenticity is about more than just honesty was a revelation for me. How about you? Consider the following questions as you explore your authentic self.

- How authentic are you as a person? As a leader?

- What is the downside to the old paradigm of heroic leadership?

- How does the new paradigm of leadership impact you? Does it resonate?

- How will this model change the way you lead in the future?

- Are you ready and willing to step forward and lead authentically?

CONCLUSION

December 1, 1955

Twenty-four days before Christmas, on December 1, 1955, on an ordinary day in Montgomery, Alabama, something extraordinary happened. Rosa Parks, a forty-two-year-old seamstress had finished a hard day at work and was looking forward to returning home for the evening. She boarded the Cleveland Avenue bus at around 6 p.m., paid her fare and sat in row eleven. The first ten rows were reserved for white passengers only. As the bus began to fill, the first ten rows were now occupied. At the next stop, Rosa and four other black passengers in row eleven were ordered to move back to make room for the boarding white riders. The driver's name was James F. Blake.

Blake and Parks had a history. Twelve years prior, in 1943, Parks had boarded the same bus with the same driver. Rosa had entered through the front door of the bus, paid her fare, and taken her seat behind row ten. Driver Blake decided to enforce city rules and instructed Parks to exit the bus and reenter through the rear door. Parks exited the bus through the front door, but before she could get back on board through the rear, Blake drove off, leaving Rosa to walk home in the rain. It was that same year, 1943, that Parks joined the

Montgomery chapter of the NAACP and became active in the civil rights movement.

Now she faced this bully again and this time he was asking her to move from her seat, to accept her "rightful" place in society. He had pushed her one too many times. Rosa remarked about her feelings that day:

> People always say that I didn't give up my seat because I was tired, but it isn't true. I was not tired physically, or no more tired than I usually was at the end of a working day. I was not old, although some people have an image of me as being old then. I was forty-two. No, the only tired I was, was tired of giving in.[1]

Rosa remained seated that day in 1955 and was arrested for her defiance. She was charged with a violation of Chapter 6, Section 11 of the Montgomery City segregation law. She never got home that night. She was bailed out of jail the next evening.

What makes a woman brave like that? She had reached the "breaking point." For forty-two years, she had experienced being treated as second class. She had watched the white children ride the bus to their new school, while the black children walked to their vastly different school facility. The bus was a symbol of the societal divide. She had been actively involved and growing in her awareness of the civil rights movement's cause.

On November 27, 1955, four days prior to her day of infamy, Rosa had been at a mass meeting in Montgomery, listening to a stirring speech by civil rights leader T. R. M. Howard. He spoke of the brutal murder earlier that year of Emmett Till in Mississippi. Perhaps his words were still stirring in Rosa's heart four days later.

For whatever reason, that day on the bus would be different. Rosa had undergone a revolution of sorts. Before she said no to James Blake, she had already experienced the beginning of change inwardly. This is where the quiet revolution happens, on the inside. A quiet revolution isn't a messy one. The violence in Watts in 1965 was a far cry from the quiet strength displayed on the Cleveland Avenue bus at 6 p.m. on a Thursday evening in Montgomery, Alabama.

COMMON GROUND — QUIET REVOLUTION

Quiet revolution is different than the reaction in Watts. While it is driven by the same internal passion and fueled by the same emotions, the outward expression and means of changing the status quo differ. The riots in Watts were a *yang* response, an aggressive, angry, tumultuous overthrow of the powers that oppress. *Yin* leaders operate from a different playbook. We have a different set of strengths that are useful in a cultural struggle, such as the one we are currently engaged in. We are uniquely positioned to move the cultural narrative by means of the pen, deep thought, and careful, calculated, wise and strategic planning.

It's not through brute force but through quiet boldness, like Rosa's, that the culture will be moved. The revolution has already begun. Will you join?

Cultural revolution is a long, arduous task that is well worth the wait and effort. What we can change more readily is ourselves. This book has laid out a map. Different than a plan or path, which implies a flow through a set of predictable stages or steps, a map is more reflective of the messiness of real life. A map is helpful to see where you are, where you need or want to go, and where you are currently headed. You can refer to a map frequently along the journey toward your intended destination, even when you get lost. The map isn't the point; arriving at your destination is. As you move toward the kind of leadership Rosa exemplified, perhaps the map in figure 17 will serve as a guide.

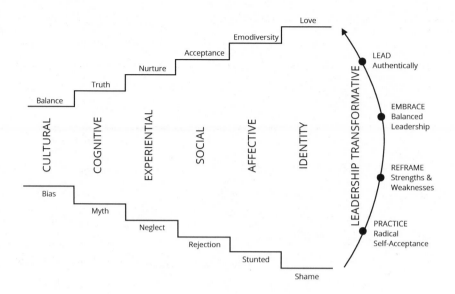

Figure 17. Introvert revolution map.

The map displays the upside and downside of six aspects of the social self. Culturally, many of us have been negatively impacted by bias at the expense of balance. Cognitively, we have been victims of myth at the expense of truth. Experientially, we have received neglect or mistreatment instead of nurture. Socially, we have been out, feeling rejection, rather than in, feeling acceptance and belonging. Affectively or emotionally, we have often been stunted rather than fully embracing our emodiversity. Lastly, for some of us, we have been marked by shame rather than love.

The downward steps show us how we may have gotten here, the negative things that may have happened to us. The upward steps show us what some have experienced and others of us have missed, the positive side of the equation. The arrow from the bottom steps back to the peak displays the journey of leadership transformation. It includes the practice of radical self-acceptance, the reframing of strengths and weaknesses, the embracing of balanced leadership, and the will and ability to lead authentically.

This map may prove to be a useful tool if you get lost and need to figure out where you are or to determine which dimension of your journey you currently need to focus on. As you move toward the ultimate end, the good life, a life of wholeness, meaning, purpose, truth, and authenticity, may this map help you find your way. Safe travels!

FINAL REFLECTION QUESTIONS

We've reached the end of our journey together, but your personal journey may be just beginning. Consider the next steps for you as an introverted leader as you reflect on the following questions.

1. Knowing what you know now, how do you feel about yourself as an introverted leader? On a scale of 1 to 10, how confident are you that you have what it takes to lead well in the future?

2. Which stage of your introverted identity development are you currently in (see Introduction, page 15)?

3. How will you work for cultural revolution? What is your plan of action? What will you do in your organization?

4. What do you want to learn more about? What additional books or articles do you want to read? What courses or seminars do you want to take?

5. How will you pursue your own personal revolution? What is your specific plan?

6. Who is going to help you on this quest? Who is "safe enough" to help you work through social pain, rejection or shame? Who are your fellow travelers?

APPENDIX A

Measuring Introversion-Extroversion

How do we measure levels of introversion or extroversion? How do we find our place on the spectrum? It's important to know that introversion-extroversion is not really a binary thing; it's a continuum. There are all kinds of unique personal patterns at every point between extreme introversion and extreme extroversion.

| Extreme Introversion | Moderate Introversion | Ambiversion | Moderate Extroversion | Extreme Extroversion |

Figure 18. Introversion-extroversion continuum.

That being the case, what is the best way to measure someone's place? There are several options available. Here are my thoughts on each:

MYERS-BRIGGS TYPE INDICATOR® (MBTI)

This is probably the most widely used instrument, speaking historically. It's been used in all kinds of organizations and governmental agencies. It has recently come under some fire with questioning of its reliability (whether its results stay the same each time you take it) and the credentials of its creators.[1] "There is just no evidence behind it," said Adam Grant, Wharton School professor. He went on to note, "The characteristics measured by the test have almost no predictive power on how happy you'll be in a situation, how you'll perform at your job, or how happy you'll be in your marriage."[2]

The MBTI yields *one of sixteen patterns* based on your result in each of four dimensions. When you take it, you might end up with my score INFJ (introverted, intuitive, feeling, judging). Each of us gets a pattern of four letters beginning with either I or E (introverted or extroverted). Though this is probably the most widely used, I would suggest using another method for assessing your place on the spectrum.

BIG FIVE INVENTORY

Beginning in the 70s and continuing to the present, there has been an attempt to create a more empirically derived assessment of enduring personality traits. Two separate research teams independently worked to differentiate these five stable traits of human personality.[3] The result of these combined teams is known as the Big Five Personality Inventory.[4] The test measures traits of individuals along five continua as follows: closed-mindedness/open-mindedness, disorganized/conscientious, introverted/extroverted, disagreeable/agreeable, neuroticism/emotional stability. If you have a hard time remembering these five traits, you can use the word OCEAN (openness, conscientiousness, extroversion, agreeableness and neuroticism) to help you.

One of my concerns with the Big Five assessment and Big Five personality theory is the likely bias toward extroversion, reflective of the cultural bias in which it was created. The Big Five, though the most widely used and most researched theory in the psychological community, has also had its critics. One of those outspoken critics was Hans Eysenck, the psychologist who posited the stimulation theory of extroversion and introversion.[5] Others have questioned the validity of the Big Five model as well.[6] Though the instrument has strong support from the psychological community, this is the same community that has pathologized sadness and fear and that has sought to include introversion among the list of personality disordered traits. The Big Five traits are not understood as values neutral, but as having healthier or pathological aspects at either end of some of the traits. Though this is an empirically validated measure, I would also suggest using a different method to see where you fall.

THE DISC® ASSESSMENT

Here's my first choice, which I use in my work with leaders and am certified in administering. The DISC is a behavioral style self-assessment (very similar but not identical to the concept of temperament) that measures patterns on four dimensions of normal human behavior. What is really important is the DISC model is based on the concept of values neutrality. That means every score is right.[7] There are no wrong scores, just different. Taking the version of DISC that I use yields *one of 384 patterns*, with a specific report connected to each of these patterns. For that reason, the DISC is much more nuanced and helpful in understanding self and others.

I've found that mastering the four dimensions of DISC, and all that can be known about someone according to those dimensions, is far easier to do as opposed to trying to gain insight from one of sixteen patterns on the MBTI, using the Big Five criteria, or remembering someone's top five of thirty-four potential strengths.[8]

THE ADVANTAGES OF DISC

From ancient times, we have noticed that people have certain tendencies in regard to the ways they behave, communicate and deal with conflict, among other things. These human traits are observable and can be categorized. William Moulton Marston wrote *Emotions of*

Normal People in 1928, in which he described four aspects of normal human behavior. Hans Eysenck also developed a personality theory that was organized around four quadrants; the theory is remarkably similar to not only Marston's model but to the four ancient Greek temperaments.[9] Bill Bonstetter, chairman and founder of TTI Success Insights, took the genius of Marston and applied it through the use of a computerized assessment to measure behavioral styles beginning in the 1980s. TTI is an industry-leading provider of the DISC assessment.

There are four dimensions of behavioral style measured with DISC. Each continuum ranges from 0 to 100. The D continuum indicates one's approach to *problems* and *challenges*. The I continuum indicates one's approach to *people* and *contacts*. The S continuum indicates one's approach to *pace* and *change*. Lastly, the C continuum indicates one's approach to *procedures* and *compliance*. So, the composite DISC score of any individual is actually the combination of four scores along four continua.

There are two distinct aspects of extroverted behavior:

D extroversion (at the high side of the D continuum) is fast-paced, results-oriented extroversion. It loves challenge and winning. It is often described with adjectives like driven or direct. This is "just do it" extroversion.

I extroversion (at the high side of the I continuum) is also fast-paced, but is more people oriented. It is optimistic, winsome, gregarious and charismatic. It is often described with adjectives like influential or inspiring. This is "be happy" extroversion.

There are also two distinct aspects of introverted behavior:

S introversion (at the high side of the S continuum) is slow-paced, people-oriented introversion. It is extremely loyal, logical and group oriented. It is often described with adjectives like steady or stable. This is "don't just do it; think about it" introversion.

C introversion (at the high side of the C continuum) is slow-paced, task-oriented introversion. It tends to be precise, detail-oriented and quality-oriented. It is often described with adjectives like compliant or correct. This is "do it right" introversion.

So, the best question is not a binary question (are you introverted or extroverted?) but a question that reflects the presence of a continuum (what kind of introvert, ambivert or extrovert are you?). Here's a way to determine that. If you plot your DISC scores along each of the four dimensions on the following chart, you can see how many of your four scores fall into relevant sections:

	D	I	S	C
75-100%	STRONG EXTROVERSION	STRONG EXTROVERSION	STRONG INTROVERSION	STRONG INTROVERSION
50-75%	MODERATE EXTROVERSION	MODERATE EXTROVERSION	MODERATE INTROVERSION	MODERATE INTROVERSION
25-50%	MODERATE INTROVERSION	MODERATE INTROVERSION	MODERATE EXTROVERSION	MODERATE EXTROVERSION
0-25%	STRONG INTROVERSION	STRONG INTROVERSION	STRONG EXTROVERSION	STRONG EXTROVERSION

Figure 19. DISC dimensions of introversion-extroversion.

The more scores that fall into the strong boxes connected to introversion or extroversion, the clearer the trait. The more scores that fall into the moderate boxes, the more the DISC results indicate an ambiverted temperament.

The DISC provides a more nuanced understanding of introversion, ambiversion and extroversion. You can also find yourself according to your two highest scores (or one singular score if it stands out alone) on this chart and begin to see what kind of introvert, extrovert or ambivert you may be.

EXTROVERT IDEAL	
D Decisive Task-Oriented Extrovert	**I** Outgoing People-Oriented Extrovert
DI Decisive Outgoing Extrovert	**ID** Outgoing Decisive Extrovert
THE EXTROVERTS	

DS Decisive Careful Ambivert	**IC** Outgoing Analytical Ambivert
SD Careful Decisive Ambivert	**CI** Analytical Outgoing Ambivert
JAZZY	
DC Decisive Analytical Ambivert	**IS** Outgoing Careful Ambivert
CD Analytical Decisive Ambivert	**SI** Careful Outgoing Ambivert
TASK	PEOPLE
THE AMBIVERTS	

S Careful People-Oriented Introvert	**C** Analytical Task-Oriented Introvert
SC Careful Analytical Introvert	**CS** Analytical Careful Introvert
THE INTROVERTS	

YIN LEADERS

Figure 20. DISC high scores and temperament.

You'll notice that the D, I, DI and ID patterns are consistent with the *extrovert ideal* in our American culture, the idea that mental health and leadership are connected to how extroverted someone is. In this paradigm, every other pattern outside of the shaded area potentially feels lacking due to the cultural bias.

The S, C, SC and CS patterns are consistent with a clear pattern of introversion. The column on the right illustrates the three kinds of ambiverts according to DISC. SD, DS, CI, IC ambiverts have dominant traits that are at odds with each other according to both introversion/extroversion and people/task orientation. This is called a "jazz" pattern. DC and CD patterns indicate task-oriented ambiversion. Many people with this pattern will experience many of the negative stereotypes around introversion. Their extroversion is task-oriented, not happy enough. You'll ordinarily not see their extroversion until there is a project under way with something to accomplish. IS and SI patterns indicate people-oriented ambiversion. These ambiverts often struggle with achieving tangible results, but certainly enjoy people and relationships.

A SECOND PICTURE

Other assessments of behavioral style (temperament, personality) only provide one result that reflects the overall natural traits of the individual. An additional benefit of using the DISC assessment is that it provides a second picture. As well as showing the natural style of the person taking the assessment, it also shows the adapted style. This is a picture of the way the person is currently behaving that may be different from his or her natural or at rest pattern. This gives us a glimpse into the way the person is trying, in some way, to be someone he or she isn't naturally, the degree to which he or she is acting. This second picture, compared to the first, is often a good conversation starter about how things are going relative to current levels of stress in the workplace.

The DISC is perhaps the best way to measure, understand and apply a more person-specific assessment of one's place on the introversion-extroversion continuum.[10] If you've never taken the DISC and are interested in taking the assessment as a way to better understand where you fall along the continuum, please contact me at andy@ price-associates.com.

APPENDIX B

Extroverts Who Get It

"Justice will not be served until those who are unaffected are as outraged as those who are."

—Benjamin Franklin (extrovert)

Most often, for culture to change, it requires those in positions of power with the privileges of dominant culture status to forego their positions or advantages for the benefit of others. In the civil rights movement, this was most definitely the case.

Consider the story of Bruce Klunder (1937–1964), a white Presbyterian minister and civil rights activist from Oregon. Shortly after his graduation from Yale, Klunder moved to Cleveland, Ohio, to take a position as the assistant executive secretary at Western Reserve University. He was married and had two small children. Identifying with the cause for racial equality, he soon became involved. Klunder opposed the construction of segregated schools by the Cleveland City School District and was willing to put his convictions into action, ultimately being run over by a bulldozer.[1] Many viewed this as the ultimate act of sacrifice for others. He is listed as one of forty names on the national Civil Rights Memorial in Montgomery, Alabama. What makes someone like Klunder become so passionate that he is willing, for the sake of others, to give up his own life?

I interviewed many *yin* leaders to gain insights for this book. One story stands out. One extroverted leader cared enough to intervene in a positive way in the life of his introverted report. She had just received her first negative evaluation from a new vice president in the organization. The criticism was filled with many typical "be more extroverted" kinds of comments. The negative feedback threw her for a loop. Enter the extrovert hero of the story. He took the time to hear her out, listen to the impact of the misplaced feedback on her sense of self, and told her emphatically that the comments weren't true and that she was just as valuable and effective as she had always been.

If you're reading this appendix (and this book), and you are an extrovert, let me begin by saying thank you. You are going out of your way to understand others who are very different than yourself. In my estimation, that's a big part of character. You may be reading this in relation to someone specific in your world, someone you really want to understand better. Or, you may be reading this in relation to fifty percent or more of your workforce who are more introverted than extroverted. In any case, not only does this make you caring, this also makes you smart. Extroverted leaders who get it ("it" being introversion) have a significant advantage in the future as opposed to those who don't.

In all great social and societal movements, there are those involved in the cause who are not part of the group they seek to lift up. Men were involved in the women's struggle. Many non-African Americans have been part of the civil rights struggle. It takes something special to push through the egocentric bias that we all have and invest time in understanding others.

I very intentionally wrote this book targeted at an introverted and ambiverted audience, non-extroverts. As a result, there will often be times that you may have rightly felt like you were reading someone else's mail, like the things I described didn't seem real. Likely, it's not what you have experienced, but if you take the time to ask someone who lives it daily, I suspect they'll confirm what I am describing at some level.

GETTING IT

When I was first introduced to Janet Helms's model of White Racial Identity in graduate school, I was a bit oblivious. "I'm not racist. I had many Asian friends in high school," I objected internally. I didn't understand how unaware I was of the advantages that had been afforded me simply because of the color of my skin. I was at stage one in Helms's model, *contact*. The most obvious characteristic of this stage is naiveté, not understanding the differences and the imbalances in power all around us. Our professor had us read a book I've never forgotten. *A Different Mirror: A History of Multicultural America* was a real eye-opener. For the first time, I began to understand history through a different lens. Author Ronald Takaki wrote:

> To become visible is to see ourselves and each other in a different mirror of history. . . . By viewing ourselves in a mirror which reflects reality, we can see our past as undistorted and no longer have to peer into our future through a glass darkly.[2]

Reading that book pushed me into stage two of Helms's model, *disintegration*.[3] The disintegration stage is characterized by anxiety, depression and guilt resulting from seeing the reality of past offenses by our race and fearing ostracism by our race in the future if we were to break our collective silence. For me, I was discovering very ugly truths about my racial heritage, things many white people want kept quiet. Helms went on to articulate four more stages of moving toward a fully mature acceptance of white racial identity. If we adapt her model to describe the journey for extroverts as they become fully aware of their extroverted identity and cultural advantages, it might look something like the following:

- Stage 1: Contact

  "We're all just people; the extrovert-introvert discussion is ridiculous; we all have pain."

- Stage 2: Disintegration

  "I'm realizing how hard it's been for introverts in our society; we extroverts haven't made it easy for them."

- Stage 3: Reintegration

  "Introverts need to stop whining and get over it; they're not persecuted."

- Stage 4: Pseudo-Independence

  "I'm beginning to think there is something to this extrovert ideal; I believe, at least in my head, that introverts might have a hard time in the United States."

- Stage 5: Immersion-Emersion

  "I've been reading Quiet *by Susan Cain and talking about it with my introverted coworkers; I'm learning a lot about what their world is like."*

- Stage 6: Autonomy

  "Introversion and extroversion are both gifts to all of us; we need both kinds of people at all levels of every organization to keep our organization and society balanced and healthy."

Healthy people will ask, "Where am I on this model?" Some extroverts are going to get it. Others aren't. Hopefully, you are part of the former group. If so, your increased empathy and understanding will serve you well as a leader and will be a godsend to introverted leaders all around you.

The funny thing about getting it is that, if you get it, you realize you don't fully get it. There are limitations on empathy. Having healthy empathy involves aspects or degrees of putting yourself in others' shoes. The reality, however, is that you can't actually be in their shoes. There is nothing more frustrating than someone saying in the midst of another's pain, "I've been there." They haven't.

For those of you who get introversion and aspects of our struggle as leaders, you also realize you will never understand it from inside. I'm white. Though I deeply empathize with the pain of other ethnicities mistreated by white people, it would be offensive for me to tell them, "I get it." I'm male. I can't tell women, "I know how you feel." I can continue to do things like read books about and listen to the accounts of the plight of these groups and their struggle for equality and dignity. But, I will never be something I'm not. The same is true for you as extroverts. Though you will never fully understand what it's like to be an introvert (or an ambivert), we appreciate you understanding our struggle as much as you are able.

NOT GETTING IT

While some extroverts will understand the issues on which this book is focused, many won't. We can't have unrealistic expectations. Many extroverts, who enjoy being on the power side of the equation in more ways than one, will not only be hesitant to share power with others but will likely be unable to even see the reality of the situation. How can this be? How can so many highly intelligent extroverted leaders not be able to see this situation accurately? The problem is bias.

Being in the in-group, the group in power, the dominant group has some common tendencies. The difference can be seen in the contrast between "mindful minorities" and "mindless majorities." In other words, "advantaged group members [extroverts], because of their superior status, pay little attention to the intergroup relationship."[4]

Symptoms of extroverts who don't get it include the following:

- Low empathy for or bias against introverts, minimizing introverts pain: "They have a 'poor me' attitude."

- Claiming to be "temperament blind" (similar to "color-blind"): "I don't see the differences. I treat everyone the same."

- Constantly advancing extroversion as the model of health or leadership.

- Pushing introverts to be more outgoing, optimistic or assertive and confident.

- Complaining about the negativity of introverts on the team.

- Refusing to adapt communication or strategies to individual temperaments.

- Ridiculing or teasing people who are less extroverted.

- Rolling their eyes in disbelief or disdain when the subject of introversion is brought up.

DO YOU GET IT?

Answer true or false to the following.

1.	Extroverts are not superior leaders to introverts.	T or F
2.	I think extroverts have many unfair advantages in Western culture.	T or F
3.	Introverts are often unfairly judged by extroverts.	T or F
4.	Introversion is a strength, not a weakness.	T or F
5.	Life is harder for introverts in the West.	T or F
6.	The social pain resulting from being rejected due to introversion is as real as the pain resulting from being rejected because of gender, ethnicity or religious preference.	T or F
7.	I obtain feedback from people I work with in different ways connected to their temperaments.	T or F
8.	I give introverts a good "heads up" in advance of changes most of the time.	T or F
9.	I'm committed to creating a team in which introverts and extroverts are uniquely valued according to their differences.	T or F
10.	Introverts in brainstorming sessions aren't talking because there is too much going on in their heads in the moment.	T or F

Add up the total of your responses. If you answered true to most of the items, you are well on your way toward being an extrovert who gets it. If you answered false to many of them, you may still have a way to go to understand the realities related to introverts you work with. Hopefully, this book will help you on that journey. Thanks again for taking the time to attempt to better understand us.

APPENDIX C

Whole Person Coaching

"I prefer to think of my patients and myself as fellow travelers, a term that abolishes distinctions between 'them' (the afflicted) and 'us' (the healers)."

—Irving Yalom

Bruce was a salesman in his previous work life. As part of a new start-up construction company, his new role included this former skill. The pressure of sales-related focus was taking a toll on him when we first met. As most introverts, Bruce detested the dreaded cold calls he was being asked to make. What he didn't realize was that in the past, he had developed a successful sales position based on his more introverted strengths of loyalty, customer service and similar qualities. Many of his sales were to repeat customers who had grown to trust his honesty and service orientation. In his new job, he was being asked to be a salesman in a different way. He was struggling with this and feeling quite a bit of stress.

He didn't know he was an introvert. The first time we sat down to look at his DISC report (low-D, low-I, high-S, high-C), we were able to have the first of many conversations focused on his behavioral style and why he struggled with the things he did. It was life changing for him to learn about introversion, who he is and why the things he struggled with weren't unique to him but common for those on his end of the spectrum. I had the privilege of walking a sacred part of Bruce's journey with him as a coach. My work with Bruce naturally included focus on both his work and personal life.

Sometimes consultants or coaches try to work with parts of people. They focus on the work part or the home part. People aren't divisible like that. People are incredibly complex. There aren't enough assessments in existence to accurately describe the nuances of each and every human being. Additionally, the commonly cited idea of work-life balance is a myth! We can't nor should we try to compartmentalize our existence into work and life. The two are woven together in one whole. What happens or doesn't happen at work affects our whole person and the same is true in our life outside of work. The lines aren't clear; they are blurry and overlap significantly. Each of us is only one indivisible person.

We're all broken! The first step toward growth is a step of honesty and self-awareness, particularly owning those aspects of self that aren't functioning as they ought. The good news here is that we are all broken and imperfect. The reality is that only some of the population agree with that statement and have the courage to be vulnerable about their struggles. In this sense, there are no whole people, just broken ones of different sorts. How can we best help broken people toward health, wholeness and authenticity?

One of the ways to grow and overcome brokenness is through the means of a therapeutic relationship, *counseling*. Many people walk through the door called counseling and into a new way of being. There are, however, a few problems with counseling. Counseling still has a *stigma*, one more thing introverts don't need, attached to it. Much counseling and psychotherapy is practiced from a pathological perspective. The perceived prevalence of depression and anxiety, exaggerated due to the diagnostic criteria, can result in over diagnosis for introverts and their *yin* emotionality. Unfortunately, due to the influence of the insurance industry, most counseling is short-term, six to eight sessions. It has taken many years to develop the patterns of thought, feeling and behavior described in this book. It will not be truly changed in six sessions.

Coaching is a newer, far less regulated field. It is offered mostly in the context of working environments. Some seek out coaching as a healthy way to further their own personal development; others desire to remedy a specific problem or behavior. It can be life changing, like counseling, but it also has a few potential problems. Most often, coaching is provided in the context of, and toward the end of, *improved performance*. Pushing performance goals prematurely with introverts who are struggling to recover from the things discussed in this book can prove to be not only ineffective but personally damaging. Limiting much of the coaching interaction and discussions to the context of work, many clients are only *half understood*. The line between the self at work and the self outside of work is a fiction. The whole person lives in all spheres of life. Working on work-related issues always connects to life outside of work and vice versa.

To provide a good balance (*he*) between counseling and coaching, the process of Whole Person Coaching is uniquely suited to the needs of introverted leaders.

WHOLE PERSON COACHING

A *dialectic* is a synthesis of two things in tension with one another that together comprise a whole. These dialectical relationships are all around us. We become the people we are as a result of both nature and nurture.[1] We are both I and we. *Yin* and *yang* is a classic example of this concept. By blending aspects of counseling and working in a coaching context, the client can be served more holistically. Whole

Person Coaching brings therapeutic understanding to the coaching process to better serve the client in the following ways:

- **No stigma.** Stigma is directly connected to the problem of shame that is addressed in this book. Introverts don't need another thing to be ashamed of. Coaching does not have the same stigma attached to it as does counseling. People don't feel as if they need to hide the fact from others that they have a coach. This is a huge advantage of working through the primary lens of coaching.

- **Wellness perspective.** To benefit from working with a coach is a healthy choice. Having a coach is not an admission of weakness. All of us are less than our potential selves, and working on self-improvement is a healthy thing to do. Coaching is done from a wellness perspective.

- **Being and doing.** Whole Person Coaching avoids the trap of dividing the person in half, as if their work self and their non-work self are not intimately connected. By emphasizing performance and bottom line, coaches often reflect the extroverted results-oriented (*yang*) bias of our culture. In reality, people are far more than what they accomplish. You aren't what you do but your actions and accomplishments often improve with the development of your being.

- **Whole person.** People have many layers of uniqueness. They also each have a unique story of the way they have gotten to where they are. A coach who is also trained and skilled in counseling theories and techniques applies all relevant knowledge of client traits and background to the process of coaching.

In many respects, the needs of *yin* leaders are the same as their extroverted counterparts. We all have blind spots and challenges that hinder us from reaching our full potential as leaders. Most of us can work to become better aligned with our workplace roles and focus. Everyone benefits from greater organizational and individual clarity. We can all seek to improve our performance and meet our personal and organizational goals. Everyone will gain from this unique relationship we call coaching.

In other ways, *yin* leaders (introverts and ambiverts) have a unique set of additional challenges in an extrovert-biased culture. Here are some of the dialectical needs related to introverted leaders that I frequently encounter:

- **Self-acceptance.** For introverts, who tend to be highly self-critical and live in a world that tells them they are inadequate, increasing their level of self-acceptance requires great patience, encouragement and an affirming relationship. Greater self-acceptance is directly correlated with improved well-being and the acceptance of others.

- **Recognition of strengths.** For many introverted leaders, their natural strengths have been devalued by themselves and others around them. Instead, focus has been placed on more highly valued extroverted strengths, things that are often challenges for introverts. Often, there is a need to reframe perceived weaknesses of introverts as actual strengths (e.g., pessimism as a valuable skill to keep the team from making mistakes).

- **Leadership confidence.** Related to both self-acceptance and strengths recognition, introverted leaders often lack confidence.

- **Leading as oneself.** In a culture that is constantly sending two messages to introverted leaders (1. Introverts can't lead. 2. You need to be extroverted.), the struggle to simply be oneself and feel comfortable in one's own skin is significant.

- **Belonging and meaning.** The psychological literature is clear. Meaning is connected to how much we feel like we are loved and belong. For introverts, who often find themselves outside of the inner circle, this can be a real struggle.

- **Leadership competency development.** Many introverted leaders will find themselves needing to improve specific workplace-related skills, including presentation skills, negotiation, interpersonal skills, conflict management and resiliency.

- **Environmental challenges.** Introversion is fundamentally about external stimulation. Oftentimes, the environment itself poses certain challenges for introverts that can be adjusted for increased engagement and results.

- **Overcoming systemic barriers.** The culture of the West and the systems within it comprise a real barrier to progress for more introverted leaders. Helping them work through or even around these barriers is helpful not only to them but to the larger systems of which they are a part.

- **Grief and loss.** From the beginning, many introverts have experienced various losses related to their temperament. This coaching relationship provides a place to process those life losses, grieve them in a healthy way, and move on toward a brighter future.

- **Shame resiliency.** Shame is toxic. Learning how to reduce the damaging effects of shame that are so prevalent among introverts is key to future confidence, assertiveness and well-being.

- **Trauma and mistreatment.** The research has indicated that an inordinate percentage of victimized people are introverted. Introverts are often the targets of workplace bullying and similar forms of mistreatment.[2]

- **Anxiety.** Introverts tend to have naturally higher levels of stimulation and proneness toward anxiety. Differentiation between healthy and unhealthy anxiety or working through anxiety that has developed in response to adverse life circumstances is part of the dialectical process of Whole Person Coaching.

Coaching is not therapy; though when performed by a coach who is also a licensed counselor, it can often include significant therapeutic insights. Being both a coach and a therapist, I am uniquely attuned to deeper psychological and systems-related issues in the coaching process.

Coaching is *yang*. It tends to focus on performance, goal-achievement, the bottom line, utilitarian and practical ends, the *hard* or *practical stuff*. Counseling is *yin*. It tends to focus on well-being, wholeness, personal and developmental ends, the *soft* or *personal stuff*.

Which matters more? For many years in the workplace, we have attempted to separate these two aspects of individuals. We've said, "Leave your personal issues at home and focus on your work." We've talked about having a good work-life balance and good boundaries between the two hemispheres of life. What we are finding is that life and people aren't built like that. We are each one person and bring that one person into all of the spheres of our existence. Work-life balance is a myth! The hard stuff and the soft stuff are interconnected. This is the brilliance of a dialectical approach like Whole Person Coaching. It focuses on both.

ACKNOWLEDGMENTS

We all stand on the shoulders of others. I am deeply indebted to those who have gone before me in this area. I would not know myself as I am beginning to, nor be able to lead authentically, were it not for your work.

To the late Carl Jung, a note of thanks for developing your own theory as distinct from Freud that would give us the categories to have this discussion. Thank you for not pathologizing introversion, for affirming the fact that health occurs along the entire continuum.

Special thanks to Adam McHugh for writing *Introverts in the Church: Finding Our Place in an Extroverted Culture*. The beginning of your book, with the description of the Christian college students' understanding (misunderstanding) of the temperament of Jesus, began it all for me. Jesus seems to have exhibited numerous introverted tendencies, despite Richard Halverson saying that God is an extrovert.

I also want to acknowledge Susan Cain for writing *Quiet*, giving your TED talks and leading the Quiet Revolution. You are an inspiration to all of us involved in the movement and have truly stepped into a moment in history. Just like Esther, I suspect you were made "for such a time as this." I'm grateful for your continuing leadership in this area.

To Laurie Helgoe, author of *Introvert Power*. Thanks for making us aware of and for fighting the bias against introversion in the DSM community (along with Nancy Ancowitz).

To Marti Olson Laney, author of *The Introvert Advantage* and *The Hidden Gifts of the Introverted Child*, your writings have helped me understand the physiology and neural aspects of introversion and brought comfort as an "innie."

To Brené Brown, one of my favorite introverted authors and speakers, for helping me solidify the core of what I've always felt connected to my introversion. Thanks for exposing the shame gremlins in my head and for teaching me helpful strategies to make my petri dish a more hostile environment for them.

To Jennifer Kahnweiler, an extrovert, who cares enough about introverted leaders to write two books (thus far) and dedicate her life to helping us grow. You are an extrovert who gets it and a great example of healthy *yang*.

To Ron Price, my extroverted former coach and current colleague, for giving me the DISC for the first time. When I met you, I was an ENFJ (or at least I thought I was). Now, I'm an SCID with much greater self-awareness.

To Justin Foster for coming up with a disruptive book title that sounds like a contradiction.

To Tim Eckstrom for helping me cathart my anger about the extrovert ideal and for encouraging me to move to the next stage of cultural identity development that is a bit less angry.

To Whit Mitchell, my dear extroverted friend and colleague, for "getting it."

To Sharon Brooks for all your efforts in facilitating webinars and events related to the revolution.

To Maryanna Young for your friendship, encouragement and support in this journey of writing and publishing. To the rest of the creative team at Aloha. To Hannah Cross, my introverted friend and project manager, for your tireless support and encouragement on this project and cause. To Stacy Ennis, my extroverted editor, for your editorial pushbacks and revisions that have made my message more communicable, impactful and a little less biased. To Jennifer Regner and Kim Foster, introverts, who gave balance (*he*) to the editing process. To Angelina Briggs for the reflective cover design. To Shiloh Shroeder and the team at Fusion Creative Works for your great work in formatting the interiors and graphics, as usual.

To those I interviewed whose stories are concealed under different identities but which nonetheless speak to our shared experiences as introverts. Your courage to tell your stories helps others to normalize their similar experiences.

To my beta readers for taking the time to read the manuscript and offer helpful comments and feedback.

To my faithful readers, supporters and followers on the blog.

To my good friends Gordy, Mitch and Scott with whom I have processed these issues for many hours. Thanks for your patience and listening.

To my late brother Tim for getting me connected to music for introverts. I miss you.

To my sister, Jen, for taking me under your wing and running interference for me in the family system. Thanks for noticing my vulnerability as a sensitive introverted child and doing something to protect me.

To my girls (and my introverted son-in-law) for supporting me through various times of adversity related to my propensity to bring drama into our family by being true to my introverted self. I love each of you and your unique personalities.

To Theo, for inspiring me to fight this fight for future generations. Whether you are ultimately introverted or extroverted, you have brought much joy into my life.

To my wife, the ambivert that she is, for continuing to listen to my droning on and on about this issue. I'm sure your D was done long ago, but for the sake of love you continue to hear me. Thank you.

To God, who makes no mistakes and saw fit to make me introverted rather than extroverted. Anything of value in this book is ultimately derived from what You have given me. S.D.G.

ABOUT THE AUTHOR

Andy Johnson is an introvert who gets introverts from the inside out. He has dedicated his life to helping introverted leaders in all spheres of life become the authentic leaders they were destined to be. Andy devotes much of his thinking, energy and focus to understanding the realities, challenges and opportunities of introverted leaders in an extroverted world. He writes regularly on related subjects on his blog, *Revolutionary Thoughts*, at www.introvertrevolution.com. You can connect with him on LinkedIn, Google+ or follow him on Twitter @andyjohnsonPA.

Andy holds a Bachelor of Architecture degree from Cal Poly State University, San Luis Obispo; a Master of Science in Community Counseling degree from Northwest Nazarene University, Nampa, Idaho; and is currently working on his PhD in industrial and organizational psychology at Grand Canyon University, Phoenix, Arizona. He is a member of the faculty at The Complete Leader (www.thecompleteleader.org) and works as an executive coach to introverted leaders and team health specialist with Price Associates, a leadership development and performance firm (www.price-associates.com). He is certified in the use of various assessments (DISC, motivators, EQ, Trimetrix HD) with TTI Success Insights, Inc. in Phoenix, Arizona.

Andy is an author, a licensed professional counselor (LPC) in the State of Idaho, a formerly licensed architect in California and Idaho, an executive coach and organizational consultant. He is married, has three grown daughters and one grandson.

WORKING WITH ANDY

Andy is a part of Price Associates, a leadership performance firm dedicated to "helping leaders grow and change their worlds." Andy provides a variety of individual, team and organizational services to his clients, including:

WHOLE PERSON COACHING

This process as described in Appendix C connects directly to the theory and pathways to change discussed in this book. Andy works one-on-one with *yin* leaders in a coaching relationship over time, using assessments to help leaders develop into the authentic selves that will best serve those they lead.

WORKSHOPS/SEMINARS

- *Yin* **Leader Workshop:** A two-day intensive workshop for introverted and ambiverted leaders aimed at raising awareness of the struggle in a *yang* culture, clarifying the true nature of introversion, finding validation and connecting with other similar leaders to reduce isolation. Workshop includes debrief of personal report including behavioral style and workplace motivator patterns.

- **Shared Victory Team Lab:** A two-day team workshop introducing models of conflict development and team health built around the introduction of three key personal areas of assessment (behavioral style, motivators and emotional intelligence). This is often the kickoff for an engagement with a team seeking cultural changes over time.

- *Yin* and *Yang* **Together, Valuing Diversity:** A one-day team training focused on understanding and appreciating the differences (behavioral style, workplace motivators, gender and others) between individuals as they learn to value each other and find balance as a team.

- **Emotional Intelligence:** A half-day team workshop introducing the concept of emotional intelligence as a key area of team health, including the discussion of results from individual personal EQ assessments.

ASSESSMENTS

Andy is a certified behaviors, motivators, emotional intelligence and Trimetrix HD analyst with TTI Success Insights (www.ttisuccessinsights.com) and provides assessments and personal reports in the following areas of measurement:

- DISC (R4 version)
- Workplace motivators
- Emotional intelligence
- Acumen capacity
- Workplace competencies

Team health and team conflict potential reports are available based on assessments derived from *Pushing Back Entropy: Moving Teams from Conflict to Health*. These reports are used as a benchmark of current levels of these critical team metrics. Future reports can then be used to assess increasing levels of progress and development.

TEAM-RELATED SERVICES

Based on his 2014 release, *Pushing Back Entropy: Moving Teams from Conflict to Health* (often including the Shared Victory Team Lab as a kickoff and team reports described), Andy works with teams over time to help them build cultures of team health and conflict prevention. Typical engagements are twelve to eighteen months and vary in scope according to specific team-related needs.

THE COMPLETE LEADER (TCL) LEADERSHIP DEVELOPMENT PROGRAM

To fill the coming leadership gap, Andy is a certified facilitator of The Complete Leader leadership development program. The typical configuration involves working with a cohort of emerging leaders over a period of eighteen months and incorporates content from *The Complete Leader*, the use of assessments and other relevant curriculum to encourage the development of future leaders. For more information, see www.thecompleteleader.org.

KEYNOTES

Andy is an engaging and passionate speaker on various themes including:

- Yin and Yang Leadership: Balanced Leadership in an Imbalanced World

- Five Myths and Five Truths about Introversion

- Introverts and Extroverts Together

- Pushing Back Entropy: Moving Teams Away from Conflict and Toward Health

- Organizational EQ: The Key to Employee Engagement

- Workplace Bullying: A Growing Problem with Invisible Injuries

- Conflicted about Conflict?

To learn more about any of these services or to inquire about partnering together, please contact Andy at *andy@price-associates.com.*

OTHER BOOKS BY ANDY JOHNSON

Reduce conflict and build health into your workplace team. Life has a few unalterable principles. Among them is the principle of entropy: the tendency for things to move toward disorder and decay unless additional energy is added into the equation. Workplace teams without fail operate, with or without our conscious awareness, according to this principle. Resisting this tendency, conflict prevention and healthy team building are two sides of the same coin. Healthy, successful, and fulfilled teams master the principles in this book to push back entropy proactively. Doing nothing guarantees things won't change.

ENDNOTES

INTRODUCTION

1. Shaun Michael Mars. "Frye, Marquette (1944–1986)," In Blackpast.org.

2. Details of the Watts Riots taken from "144 Hours in August 1965," in *Violence in the City: An End or a Beginning?*, accessed March 31, 2015, www.usc.edu/libraries/archives/cityinstress/mccone/part4.html, and "Martin Luther King, Jr. and the Global Freedom Struggle—Watts Rebellion (Los Angeles, 1965)," accessed March 15, 2015, www.mlk-kpp01.stanford.edu.

3. Rodney Jacobs, *Race, Media and the Crisis of Civil Society: From Watts to Rodney King* (New York: Cambridge University Press, 2000), 72.

4. Susan Cain, *Quiet: The Power of Introverts in a World Where People Can't Stop Talking* (New York: Crown Publishing Group, 2012). She also calls this the "myth of the charismatic leader," drawing on the work of Warren Susman, *Culture as History: The Transformation of American Society in the Twentieth Century* (Washington DC: Smithsonian Institution Press, 2003), who traces the historical shift from a culture of character to a culture of personality.

5. S. Alexander Haslam, Stephen D. Reicher and Michael J. Platow, *The New Psychology of Leadership: Identity, Influence and Power* (New York: Psychology Press, 2011).

6. This book is intended for introverted and ambiverted leaders, all leaders who don't fit the extroverted leadership stereotype. Ambiversion is simply the middle ground between introversion and extroversion. Throughout the rest of the book, ambiverted leaders will need to appropriately adapt my descriptions of introversion to see what fits and what doesn't.

7. Brian Little, *Me, Myself and Us: The Science of Personality and the Art of Well-Being* (New York: Public Affairs, 2014). Fifty percent is a conservative estimate. Others place the preponderance of the evidence connected to the source of introversion on hereditary factors.

8. Atkinson, Morten and Sue's Racial and Cultural Identity Model. See Donald R. Atkinson, ed., *Counseling American Minorities: A Cross Cultural Perspective*, 6th ed. (New York: McGraw-Hill Companies, 2004).

CHAPTER 1. CULTURE

1. Many outrageous stage performers in the genre of heavy metal are actually introverts. This is true of most stage actors as well. What we see in concert may well be their alter ego, their inner extrovert coming out for the show. When the lights go out and the smoke clears, we may find an introvert worn out from expending so much energy, in need of a good night's rest. See Scott Barry Kaufman, "After the Show: The Many Faces of the Performer," *Psychology Today*, posted in *Beautiful Minds*, August 25, 2010, psychologytoday.com.

2. The betta fish (*betta splendens*) is also known as a "Siamese fighting fish." The males of the species are known to be very aggres-

sive (*yang*) and need to be kept in separate tanks so they don't kill each other.

3. Hazel Markus and Alana Conner, *Clash! 8 Cultural Conflicts that Make Us Who We Are* (New York: Hudson Street Press, 2013), xix.

4. Jeffrey Kauffman, *Loss of the Assumptive World: A Theory of Traumatic Loss* (New York: Brunner-Routledge, 2002), 1.

5. The formal study of values, axiology, is the work of Robert S. Hartman, who differentiates between systemic, extrinsic and intrinsic valuations of things or people. See www.hartmaninstitute.org.

6. See Brené Brown, *Daring Greatly: How the Courage to Be Vulnerable Transforms the Way We Live, Love, Parent, and Lead* (New York: Gotham Books, 2012).

7. S. Paulson, D. Chalmers, D. Kahneman, L. Santos, and N. Schiff, "The Thinking Ape: The Enigma of Human Consciousness," *Annals of the New York Academy of Science*, 1303, no. 1 (2013): 4–24.

8. See Carol Tavris and Elliot Aronson, *Mistakes Were Made (But Not By Me): Why We Justify Foolish Beliefs, Bad Decisions, and Hurtful Acts* (New York: Houghton Mifflin Harcourt, 2007).

9. See Margaret Heffernan, *Willful Blindness: Why We Ignore the Obvious at Our Peril* (New York: Walker Publishing Company, 2011).

10. The most current Myers-Briggs demographic data shows that less than half of the U.S. population is E versus I. Extroversion-introversion is not a binary trait. In reality, the number of clearly extroverted people in the population (neither introverted nor ambiverted) is probably less than twenty-five percent. This small vocal minority can be shown to have created and maintained our dominant cultural paradigm. See Laurie Helgoe, *Introvert Power: Why Your Inner Life Is Your Hidden Strength* (Naperville, IL: Sourcebooks, 2008).

11. From the title of her book, *Quiet*.

12. Mihaly Csikszentmihalyi, *Finding Flow: The Psychology of Engagement with Everyday Life* (New York: Basic Books, 1997), 6.

13. The United States is rated at 40 on a scale of 100, which means that we have a slight leaning toward the egalitarian versus the hierarchal side of the continuum. See www.geert-hofstede.com.

CHAPTER 2. YANG

1. Mohannad Al-Haj Ali, "Steve Jobs Is a Biological Arab-American with Roots in Syria," *Ya Libnan*, February 28, 2011, http://yalibnan.com.

2. Shirin Sadeghi, "Steve Jobs Was an Arab American," *New America Media*, Oct. 5, 2011, www.newamericamedia.org/author/shirin-sadeghi/.

3. Walter Isaacson, *Steve Jobs* (New York: Simon & Schuster, 2011), 112. Kindle edition.

4. Ibid, 117.

5. Tony Fang, "Yin Yang: A New Perspective on Culture," *Management and Organizational Review*, 8, no. 1 (2011): 25.

6. Ibid. See also Robin Wang, "Understanding of Yin Yang," *Religion Compass*, 7/6 (2013): 214–224; Hsaing-Ju Chen, Yuan-Hui Tsai, Shen-Ho Chang, and Kuo-Hsiung Lin, "Bridging the Systematic Thinking Gap Between East and West: An Insight into the Yin-Yang-Based System Theory," *Systemic Practice and Action Research*, 23 (2010): 173–189.

7. George Box, "Robustness in the Strategy of Scientific Model Building," in *Robustness in Statistics*, ed. R. L. Launer and G. W. Wilkinson, (New York: Academic Press, 1979): 201–236.

8. Carlin Flora, "The Pursuit of Happiness," *Psychology Today*, January 1, 2009, https://www.psychologytoday.com/articles/200812/the-pursuit-happiness.

9. Carolyn Gregoire, "How Happiness Became a Cultural Obsession." *Huffington Post*, March 20, 2014, http://www.huffingtonpost.com/2014/03/20/happiness-self-help_n_4979780.html.

10. This is not to invalidate the legitimate use of medication for those who legitimately suffer and can benefit from psychopharmaceutical intervention.

11. Oliver Burkeman, *The Antidote: Happiness for People Who Can't Stand Positive Thinking* (London: Faber & Faber, 2012).

12. Ibid.

13. Brown, *Daring Greatly*, 18.

14. The U.S. score on individualistic (as opposed to collectivistic) is 91 out of 100. See www.geert-hofstede.com.

15. Harry C. Triandis, and Michele J. Gelfand, "A Theory of Individualism and Collectivism," in *Handbook of Theories of Social Psychology* (Thousand Oaks, CA: Sage, 2012), www.gelfand.umd.edu /Individualism%20and%20Collectivism.pdf.

16. Hazel R. Markus, and Shinobu Kitayama, "Culture and the Self: Implications for Cognition, Emotion, and Motivation," *Psychological Review*, 98, no. 2 (1991): 224–253.

17. This is largely the goal of Western psychology. A healthy individual is seen as one who is able to individuate, separate from his or her family of origin, and become an independent, autonomous adult.

18. This is also the goal of Western marketing and branding, differentiating oneself from the market and the competition, standing out from the group.

19. Hugh McKay, *The Good Life: What Makes a Life Worth Living?* (Sydney, Australia: Macmillan Australia, 2013): loc. 116/4841.

20. Richard Eckersley, "A New Narrative of Young People's Health and Well-Being," *Journal of Youth Studies*, 14, no. 5 (2011), as quoted in McKay, *The Good Life.*.

21. Eric G. Wilson, *Against Happiness: In Praise of Melancholy* (New York: Sarah Crichton Books, 2008).

CHAPTER 3. YIN

1. Isaacson, *Steve Jobs*, 123.

2. Fang, "Yin Yang."

3. William Moulton Marston, *Emotions of Normal People* (Scottsdale, AZ: Target Training International, 2012).

4. Havelock Ellis, *The Dance of Life* (Cambridge, MA: The Riverside Press, 1923).

5. Ben Wener, "The Forgotten Festival: Remembering US '82 and '83 as Steve Wozniak's Dream Bash Turns 30," *The Orange County Register*, August 31, 2012, http://ocregister.com.

6. Markus and Kitayama, "Culture and the Self".

7. Simon Sinek, *Start with Why: How Great Leaders Inspire Everyone to Take Action* (New York: Penguin Group, 2011), 227.

CHAPTER 4. AND

1. Simon Sinek, *Leaders Eat Last: Why Some Teams Pull Together and Others Don't* (New York: Penguin Group, 2014).

2. Jim Collins and Jerry Porras, *Built to Last: Successful Habits of Visionary Companies* (New York: HarperCollins, 1994): 44.

3. The Hebrew word shalom is also often translated into English as "peace." Hebrew scholars believe this is an unfortunate translation. *Shalom*, similarly to *he*, means "completeness, wholeness" or "things being the way they ought to be." These two eastern languages point to a common shared idea underlying both.

4. Fang, "Ying Yang," 34.

5. Reid Hoffman and Ben Casnocha, *The Start-Up of You: Adapt to the Future, Invest in Yourself and Transform Your Career* (New York: Crown Publishing, 2012), loc 998 of 2828. Kindle version.

6. Markus and Connor, *Clash!*, xvii.

7. Richard I. Evans, "Conversations with Carl Jung," transcripts of the 1957 film published at *The Gnostic Society Library*, http://gnosis.org/Evans-Jung-Interview/evans4.html.

8. See Genesis 4:1–8.

9. I have previously called this principle entropy: a process of degradation or running down or a trend to disorder, chaos, disorganization or randomness. Some religious readers may call this "fallenness." See Andy Johnson, *Pushing Back Entropy: Moving Teams from Conflict to Health* (Nampa, ID: Restoration Publishing, 2014).

CHAPTER 5. FICTIONS & FACTS

1. Bernardo Carducci and Philip Zimbardo, "Are You Shy?" *Psychology Today*, 28, no. 6 (1995): 34-47.

2. Little, *Me, Myself and Us*.

3. This has particularly been true since the creation of the DSM-III in 1980.

4. Go to the homepage for the Centers for Medicare and Medicaid Services, ICD-9 Code Lookup, Accessed at http://cms.gov. Codes given above are ICD-9. ICD-10, the latest version, has adjusted the numerical codes but continues to see introversion as diagnosable.

5. See Nancy Ancowitz and Laurie Helgoe, "A Giant Step Backwards for Introverts," *Psychology Today*, posted by Nancy Ancowitz in *Self-Promotion for Introverts*, August 6, 2010, https://www.psychologytoday.com/blog/self-promotion-introverts/201008/giant-step-backward-introverts.

6. For more on this cultural pathologizing of *yin* emotions, see chapters eight and nine.

7.   Answers to the quiz:

1. The correct answer is d. 50%. Isabel Briggs Myers put out some incorrect information based on a guess in 1957 that 25-33% of the U.S. population was introverted. MBTI data from 2001 reflects 57% introverts in the population.

2. The correct answer is d. 40%. According to Del Jones, "Not All Successful CEOs Are Extroverts," *USA Today*, June 7, 2006, www.usatoday30.usatoday.com.

3. The correct answer is a. introverts. See Adam Grant, Francesca Gino, and David Hofmann, "Reversing the Extroverted Leadership Advantage: The Role of Employee Proactivity," *Academy of Management Journal*, 2011, 54(3), 528–550.

4. The correct answer is b. extroverts. Ibid.

5. The correct answer is b. false. See Susan Cain, *Quiet*.

6. The correct answer is b. false. See EEOC guidelines at www.eeoc.gov.

7. The correct answer is b. ambiverts. See Daniel Pink, *To Sell Is Human: The Surprising Truth About Moving Others* (New York: Riverhead Books, 2012).

8. The correct answer is c. 60%. See Linda Silverman, "Parenting Young Gifted Children," in *Intellectual Giftedness in Young Children*, ed. J. R. Whitmore (New York: The Haworth Press, 1986).

9. The correct answer is a. Ben Franklin.

10. The correct answer is c. Donald Trump.

8. The key to understanding this concept was given to me by Dr. Brian Little of Oxbridge, who derived it from the arousal theory of Hans Eysenck. See Dr. Brian Little, "Confessions of a Passionate Introvert," TED video, 18:22, posted May 17, 2014, http://tedxtalks.ted.com/video/Confessions-of-a-Passionate-Int.

9. Neural pathways are derived from Marti Olson Laney in *The Introvert Advantage: How to Thrive in an Extrovert World* (New York: Workman Publishing, 2002), who simplified the two neural paths from the findings of the 1999 positron emission tomography (PET) study of Debra Johnson, John Wiebe, Sherri Gold, Nancy Andreasen, Richard Hichwa, Leonard Watkins and Laura Boles Ponto, *American Journal of Psychiatry, 156*(2), 252–257.

10. Marti Olson Laney, *The Hidden Gifts of the Introverted Child: Helping Your Child Thrive in an Extroverted World* (New York: Workman Publishing, 2005).

CHAPTER 6. NATURE & NURTURE

1. Laney, *Hidden Gifts*.

2. Jay Belsky and Michael Pluess, "The Nature (and Nurture?) of Plasticity in Early Human Development," *Perspectives on Psychological Science*, 4, no, 4 (2009): 345–351.

3. Daniel J. Siegel and Mary Hartzell, *Parenting from the Inside Out: How a Deeper Self-Understanding Can Help You Raise Children Who Thrive* (New York: Penguin Group, 2004), 36.

4. Dr. Rohner heads up the Center for Interpersonal Acceptance and Rejection Theory at the University of Connecticut. See www.csiar.uconn.edu.

5. See Robert R. McCrae, Paul T. Costa, Fritz Ostendorf, Alois Algleitner, Martina Hrebickova, Maria D. Avia, Jesus Sanz et al., "Nature Over Nurture: Temperament, Personality, and Life

Span Development," *Journal of Personality and Social Psychology*, 78, no. 1 (2000): 173–186.

6. Actual case notes from my mother's Adult Education Pre-School class (1969).

7. Jill D. Burruss and Lisa Kaenzig, "Introversion: The Often Forgotten Factor Impacting the Gifted," *Virginia Association for the Gifted Newsletter,* 21, no. 1 (1999).

8. Noam Shpancer, "What Doesn't Kill You Makes You Weaker: A History of Hardship Is Not a Life Asset," *Psychology Today*, posted in *Insight Therapy* on August 21, 2010. https://www.psychologytoday .com/blog/insight-therapy/201008/what-doesnt-kill-you-makes-you-weaker.

9. The ACE (Adverse Childhood Experiences) study is a nationwide examination of the associations between childhood maltreatment or neglect and later-life health and well-being. For more information, see www.acestudy.org.

10. Susan Cain is a champion in this area. Beginning with her wise questioning of the configuration of school classrooms and moving into the corporate sphere in her consulting work with Steelcase, she is attempting to directly improve the work environment of thousands of introverted students and workers. See her collection at http://www.steelcase.com/en/products/category/architectural/archwalls/via/pages/quiet-spaces.aspx.

11. Lindsey Kaufman, "Google Got It Wrong: The Open-Office Trend Is Destroying the Workplace," *The Washington Post*, December 30, 2014, http://washingtonpost.com.

CHAPTER 7. BEING IN & BEING OUT

1. Roy F. Baumeister and Mark R. Leary, "The Need to Belong: Desire for Interpersonal Attachments as a Fundamental Human Motivation," *Psychological Bulletin*, 117, no. 3 (1995): 497–529.

2. His sample of self-actualized people included Abraham Lincoln, Thomas Jefferson, Albert Einstein, Eleanor Roosevelt, Jane Addams, William James, Albert Schweitzer, Aldous Huxley and Baruch Spinoza.

3. Pamela Rutledge, "Social Networks: What Maslow Misses," *Psychology Today*, posted in Positively Media, November 8, 2011, https://www.psychologytoday.com/blog/positively-media/201111/social -networks-what-maslow-misses-0.

4. Used with permission.

5. C. S. Lewis, "The Inner Ring," in *The Weight of Glory and Other Addresses* (San Francisco: Harper Collins, 2001), 146.

6. Tyler Stillman, Roy Baumeister, Nathaniel Lambert, A. Will Crescioni, C. Nathan DeWall, and Frank Fincham, "Alone and Without Purpose: Life Loses Meaning Following Social Exclusion," *Journal of Experimental Social Psychology*, 45, no. 1 (2009): 686.

7. Geoff MacDonald and Mark R. Leary, "Why Does Social Exclusion Hurt? The Relationship between Social and Physical Pain," *Psychological Bulletin*, 131, no. 2 (2005): 202–223.

8. Among the areas that light up are the anterior cingulate cortex (ACC) and the periaqueductal gray (PAG).

9. See also Naomi I. Eisenberger, "The Pain of Social Disconnection: Examining the Shared Neural Underpinnings of Physical and Social Pain," *Nature Reviews Neuroscience*, 13, no. 6 (2012): 421–434.

CHAPTER 8. GROWTH & LOSS

1. C. S. Lewis, *The Four Loves* (New York: Harcourt, 1960), 121.

2. Pauline Boss, *Ambiguous Loss: Learning to Live with Unresolved Grief* (Cambridge, MA: Harvard University Press, 1999), 11.

3. As cited in Laurie Helgoe, *Introvert Power: Why Your Hidden Life Is Your Hidden Strength*, 2nd ed. (Naperville, IL: Sourcebooks, 2013): 63.

4. Allan V. Horowitz and Jerome C. Wakefield, *The Loss of Sadness: How Psychiatry Transformed Normal Sorrow into Depressive Disorder* (New York: Oxford University Press, 2007).

5. L. S. Radloff, "The CES-D Scale: A Self-Report Depression Scale for Research in the General Population," *Applied Psychological Measurement*, 1, no. 1 (1977): 385–401.

6. Jesse Fox and K. Dayle Jones, "DSM-5 and Bereavement: The Loss of Normal Grief?," *Journal of Counseling and Development*, 91, no. 1 (2013): 113–119.

7. Horowitz and Wakefield, *Loss of Sadness*.

8. This is a reference to the science fiction movie *The Stepford Wives*. If you want to see a society that has eliminated all forms of sadness and has implemented the happy side of the extrovert ideal, watch this classic 1975 film.

CHAPTER 9. SEEING & FEELING

1. If you're also male, you may have another cultural handicap in the form of a degree of emotional underdevelopment. Our gender stereotypes teach boys not to cry or to express vulnerability. We teach them harmful slogans such as, "Big boys don't cry." Boys are culturally conditioned to channel many other emotions into the one acceptable male emotion, anger. But for introverts, openly expressing anger is rare.

2. P. Shaver, J. Schwartz, D. Kirson, and C. O'Connor, "Emotional Knowledge: Further Exploration of a Prototype Approach," in *Emotions in Social Psychology: Essential Readings*, ed. G. Parrott (Philadelphia, PA: Psychology Press, 2001): 26–56.

3. Joseph Stromberg, "The Microscopic Structures of Dried Human Tears: Photographer Rose-Lynn Fisher Captures Tears of Grief,

Joy, Laughter and Irritation in Extreme Detail," *Smithsonian*, November 19, 2013, http://smithsonianmag.com.

4. Introverts, generally experience fewer accidents because of this cautiousness, which lowers their risk of injury.

5. Alan Horwitz and Jerome Wakefield, *All We Have to Fear: Psychiatry's Transformation of Natural Anxieties into Mental Disorder* (New York: Oxford University Press, 2012). I would speculate that a large percentage of that half of the population being pathologized fall on the introverted side of the spectrum. More studies need to be done to connect the prevalence of anxiety among introverts in the population.

6. Ibid, 33.

7. Todd Kashdan and Robert Biswas-Diener, *The Upside of Your Dark Side: Why Being Your Whole Self—Not Just Your "Good" Self—Drives Success and Fulfillment* (New York: Hudson Street Press, 2014).

8. Ed Diener, Richard Lucas, and Christie Scollon, "Beyond the Hedonic Treadmill: Revising the Adaptation Theory of Well-Being," *American Psychologist*, 61, no. 4 (2006): 305–314.

9. Jordi Quoidbach, Jane Gruber, Moira Mikolajczak, Alexsandr Kogan, Ilios Kotsou, and Michael I. Norton, "Emodiversity and the Emotional Ecosystem," *Journal of Experimental Psychology: General*, 143, no. 6 (December 2014), 2057–2066, doi:10.1037/a0038025.

10. Kashdan and Biswas-Diener, *Upside of Your Dark Side*.

11. Leslie Greenberg and Sandra Paivio, "Varieties of Shame Experience in Psychotherapy," *Gestalt Review*, 1, no. 3 (1997): 205–220.

12. Jenna Goudreau, "So Begins a Quiet Revolution of the 50 Percent," *Forbes*, January 30, 2012, http://forbes.com.

CHAPTER 10. SHAME & DETOX

1. Greenberg and Paivio, "Varieties of Shame".

2. Items 5 and 6 are taken from Curtis Levang, "Shame Indicator," in *Looking Good Outside, Feeling Bad Inside: Freedom from the Shame That Hides the Real You* (Seattle, WA: YWAM Publishing, 1996).

3. If you struggle with shame connected to your introversion, I strongly suggest reading, listening to and watching everything Brené Brown has on the topic. She is by far the foremost expert on the topic. Her personal website is www.brenebrown.com.

4. Greenberg and Paivio, "Varieties of Shame."

5. Heidi LaBash and Anthony Papa, "Shame and PTSD Symptoms," *Psychological Trauma: Theory, Research, Practice, and Policy*, 6, no. 2 (2014): 159–166.

6. See figure 12, p. 123.

7. Brené Brown, *Daring Greatly*, 68.

8. K. Jessica Van Vliet, "Shame and Resilience in Adulthood: A Grounded Theory Study," *Journal of Counseling Psychology*, 55, no. 2 (2008): 233–245.

9. See Gershen Kaufman, "The Meaning of Shame: Toward a Self-Affirming Identity," *Journal of Counseling Psychology*, 21, no. 6 (1974): 568–574. Kaufman explained that shame experiences are largely nonverbal because our earliest shame-inducing experiences occurred before we had developed verbal capacity.

10. These are the opposite of the extroverts who get it mentioned in Appendix B.

CHAPTER 11. REJECTION & ACCEPTANCE

1. *U.S. History*, "51e. Japanese-American internment," http://www.ushistory.org/us/51e.asp.

2. Brian Little, *Me, Myself and Us*.

3. Brian Eckert, "Why Introverts Make Great Entrepreneurs—Plus 5 Tips for the Entrepreneurial Introvert," *Bplans*, accessed March 31, 2015, http://articles.bplans.com/author/brian-eckert.

4. Gershen Kaufman, "The Meaning of Shame: Toward a Self-Affirming Identity," *Journal of Counseling Psychology*, 21, no. 6 (1974): 568.

CHAPTER 12. STRENGTHS & WEAKNESSES

1. Emma Seppala, "What Bosses Gain by Being Vulnerable," *Harvard Business Review*, December 11, 2014, https://hbr.org/2014/12/what-bosses-gain-by-being-vulnerable.

2. Ron Price and Randy Lisk, *The Complete Leader: Everything You Need to Become a High-Performing Leader* (Boise, ID: Aloha Publishing), 15. I'm part of the faculty for The Complete Leader, a leadership development program aimed at filling the coming leadership gap in the American workplace. For more information about the program, see www.thecompleteleader.org.

3. John Geier as quoted at http://discprofiles4u.com.

4. Price and Lisk, *Complete Leader*, 21.

5. Brené Brown, *Daring Greatly*.

6. Seppala, "What Bosses Gain.".

7. David Mielach, "5 Business Tips from Albert Einstein," *Business News Daily*, April 18, 2012, http://businessnewsdaily.com.

8. See www.thepowerofintroverts.com or www.quietrev.com.

9. We actually process lots of information and lay down much long-term memory while we sleep. This explains why many introverts report often waking up with deep insights into problems first thing in the morning.

10. Arnold Henjum, "Introversion: A Misunderstood 'Individual Difference' Among Students," *Education*, 103, no. 1 (1982): 39–43.

11. Ibid.

12. Margarita Tartakovsky, "7 Persistent Myths about Introverts & Extroverts," *Psych Central* (2013), accesssed February 18, 2015, from http://psychcentral.com/blog/archives/2013/09/11/7-persistent-myths-about-introverts-extroverts/.

13. Video interview with Sarfraz Manzoor, "Malcolm Gladwell: Speaking Is Not an Act of Extroversion," *The Guardian*, posted June 21, 2010, http://theguardian.com.

14. See Amy Cuddy, "Your Body Language Shapes Who You Are," filmed June 2012, TEDGlobal video, 21:02, http://www.ted.com/talks/amy_cuddy_your_body_language_shapes_who_you_are?language=en#t-90704.

15. We normally recommend to coaching clients that seventy percent of their energy be focused on developing strengths, while only thirty percent be focused on neutralizing weaknesses.

16. Donna Owens, "Quiet Time: The Value of Introverts in the Workplace Is Often Underestimated," *HR Magazine*, 58, no. 12 (2013): 26–27.

17. Richard Waters, "Reid Hoffman, Mr LinkedIn: Reid Hoffman, the Co-founder of LinkedIn, on Why the Future Belongs to the Networkers," *FT Magazine*, March 17, 2012, ft.com.

18. What we do know from the data from TTI Success Insights, Inc., is that the one factor that seems to predict sales success is not a behavioral or temperamental factor. The workplace motivator of utilitarianism, a focus on ROI, is strongly connected to success in the sales arena. This motivation is more a reflection of a *yang* orientation, but can be found in individuals across the introvert-extrovert continuum.

19. Adam Grant, "5 Myths about Introverts and Extroverts at Work," *Huffington Post*, February 18, 2014, http://www.huffingtonpost.com/adam-grant/5-myths-about-introverts_b_4814390.html.

20. Daniel Pink, *To Sell Is Human: The Surprising Truth about Moving Others* (New York: Penguin Books, 2012).

21. See Nancy Ancowitz, *Self-Promotion for Introverts: The Quiet Guide to Getting Ahead* (New York: McGraw Hill, 2010).

22. Matthew D. Lieberman and Robert Rosenthal, "Why Introverts Can't Always Tell Who Likes Them: Multitasking and Nonverbal Decoding," *Journal of Personality and Social Psychology*, 80, no. 2 (2001): 294–310.

23. In general, only high-D extroverts "like" conflict. Some of them see it as a competition in which they can win.

24. John Brandon, "Introverts' 6 Biggest Management Challenges," *Inc.*, February 25, 2014, http://www.inc.com/john-brandon/introverts-6-biggest-management-challenges.html.

25. The current twenty-five competencies measured by *The Complete Leader* and TTI Success Insights in the Trimetrix® HD assessment are widely accepted in the industry as the most identifiable traits of leaders. This list may change over time as we continue to identify and correct biases toward extroversion in the culture that impact and are reflected in our current assessment tools.

CHAPTER 13. LEADERS & BALANCE

1. "The Declaration of Independence," *The Library of Congress*, accessed March 31, 2015, www.loc.gov.

2. Apparently, Jefferson's first draft was even stronger, addressing issues such as slavery.

3. Elaine N. Aron, *The Highly Sensitive Person: How to Thrive When the World Overwhelms You* (New York: Three Rivers Press, 1998), 17–18.

4. Adam M. Grant, Francesca Gino, and David A. Hofmann, "Reversing the Extroverted Leadership Advantage: The Role of the Employee Proactivity," *Academy of Management Journal*, 54, no. 3 (2011): 528–550.

5. Luke McCormack and David Mellor, "The Role of Personality in Leadership: An Application of the Five-Factor Model in the Australian Military," *Military Psychology*, 14, no. 3 (2002): 179–197.

6. See Christopher Gould and Len Lecci, "Leadership and Personality: What the NEO Five-Factor Inventory Tells Us," *The Department Chair*, 21, no. 3 (2011): 16–18, where a negative correlation between extroversion and leadership effectiveness was observed.

7. U.S. Bureau of Labor Statistics data in Virtuali and New Leaders Council, "Engaging Millenials Through Leadership Development, accessed March 31, 2015, www.govirtuali.com.

8. Jennifer Kahnweiler, "Introverted Leaders: The Right Mentors for Millennials," guest post at Ryan Jenkins, *Next Generation Catalyst* (blog), November 12, 2012, www.ryan-jenkins.com.

9. John Boitnott, "Dear CEO: This Is Why Millenials Don't Want to Work for You," *Inc.* August 22, 2014, http://www.inc.com/john-boitnott/dear-ceo-this-is-why-millennials-don-t-want-to-work-for-you.html.

10. Eckert, "Why Introverts Make Great Entrepreneurs."

11. Henjum, "Introversion.".

12. David A. Heenan and Warren Bennis, "The Case for Co-Leaders," in *Business Leadership*, ed. Rob Brandt and Tamara Kastl (San Francisco: Jossey-Bass: 2003): 140.

13. Peter F. Drucker, "Leadership as Work" in *The Essential Drucker: The Best of Sixty Years of Peter Drucker's Essential Writings on Management* (New York: Collins Business, 2001).

CHAPTER 14. AUTHENTICITY & LEADERSHIP

1. Doug Conant, foreword to *The Introverted Leader: Building on Your Quiet Strength*, by Jennifer Kahnweiler (San Francisco: Berrett-Koehler Publishers, 2013): x.

2. Reid Hoffman, the co-founder of LinkedIn, discusses the problem inherent in our hero-obsessed culture. See his LinkedIn post, "Why Relationships Matter: I-to-the-we," November 6, 2012, www.linkedin.com.

3. Bill George, *True North: Discover Your Authentic Leadership* (San Francisco: Jossey-Bass, 2007): xxxiii.

4. Mike Robbins, "The Power of Authenticity," *TEDx Greenbrook School*, May 21, 2013, www.youtube.com.

5. See Brené Brown, *Daring Greatly*.

6. Drucker, "Leadership as Work."

7. Ron Price, *The Complete Leader* slides.

8. Hoffman, "Why Relationships Matter."

9. Ibid.

10. Donovan Campbell, *The Leader's Code: Mission, Character, Service, and Getting the Job Done* (New York: Random House, 2013), xiii–xv.

11. Peter Shankman, *Nice Companies Finish First: Why Cutthroat Management Is Over—and Collaboration Is In* (New York: Palgrave Macmillan, 2013).

12. Haslam, Reicher, and Platow, *The New Psychology of Leadership.* (New York: Psychology Press, 2011).

13. The removal of all hierarchy and titles under the direction of the *yin* leader Tony Hsieh at Zappos.com is an example of this radical paradigm shift. Hsieh calls this modified structure a holacracy.

CONCLUSION

1. Rosa Parks and James Haskins, *Rosa Parks: My Story* (Dial Books, 1992): 116.

APPENDIX A:
MEASURING INTROVERSION-EXTROVERSION

1. Joseph Stromberg, "Why the Myers-Briggs Test Is Totally Meaningless," *Vox*, July 15, 2104, http://www.vox.com/2014/7/15/5881947/myers-briggs-personality-test-meaningless.

2. Adam Grant, "Say Goodbye to MBTI: The Fad That Won't Die," *LinkedIn*, posted September 17, 2013, www.linkedin.com. See also http://bizcatalyst360.com/why-the-myers-briggs-test-is-totally-meaningless/.

3. Paul Costa and Robert McCrae worked together at the National Institutes of Health. Warren Norman, University of Michigan, and Lewis Goldberg, University of Oregon, also collaborated.

4. See O. P. John and S. Srivastava, ed., "The Big Five Trait Taxonomy: History, Measurement, and Theoretical Perspectives," in *Handbook of Personality: Theory and Research*, 2nd ed. (New York: Guilford, 1999): 102–138. See also O. P. John, L. P. Naumann, and C. J. Soto, "Paradigm Shift to the Integrative Big-Five Trait Taxonomy: History, Measurement, and Conceptual Issues," *Handbook of Personality: Theory and Research*, (ed.) O. P. John, R. W. Robins, and L. A. Pervin (New York: Guilford Press, 2008): 114–158. See also http://fetzer.org.

5. See Hans Eysenck, "Four Ways Five Factors Are Not Basic," *Personality and Individual Differences*, 13, no. 6 (1992): 667–673.

6. Jack Block, "A Contrarian View of the Five-Factor Approach to Personality Description," *Psychological Bulletin*, 117, no. 2 (1995): 187–215.

7. This is a key difference from the Big Five paradigm of personality traits.

8. The Gallup organization has been successful in their effort to promote the use of the StrengthsFinder assessment in the organizational world. StrengthsFinder does not measure introversion or extroversion per se (although some of the strengths

would certainly be connected to the construct of introversion: *analytical, consistency, includer, responsibility*).

9.   See Hans Eysenck, "Genetic and Environmental Contributors to Individual Differences: The Three Major Dimensions of Personality," *Journal of Personality*, 58, no. 1 (1990): 245–261.

10.   For more on the DISC model, see Johnson, *Pushing Back Entropy* and Appendix A: Behavioral Styles (How).

APPENDIX B: EXTROVERTS WHO GET IT

1.   "Martyrs Remembered: Bruce Klunder," *Southern Poverty Law Center*, accessed March 31, 2015, http://splcenter.org.

2.   Patrick Takaki, *A Different Mirror: A History of Multicultural America* (New York: Little, Brown, 1993): 426.

3.   David M. Tokar and Jane L. Swanson, "An Investigation of the Validity of Helms's (1984) Model of White Racial Identity Development," *Journal of Counseling Psychology*, 38, no. 3 (1991): 296–301.

4.   Stephen C. Wright and Donald M. Taylor, "The Social Psychology of Cultural Diversity: Social Stereotyping, Prejudice and Discrimination," in *The SAGE Handbook of Social Psychology: Concise Student Edition*, (ed.) Michael A. Hogg and Joel Cooper (Thousand Oaks, CA: SAGE, 2007): 372.

APPENDIX C: WHOLE PERSON COACHING

1.   Arnold Sameroff, "A Unified Theory of Development: A Dialectical Integration of Nature and Nurture," *Child Development*, 81, no. 1 (2010): 6–22.

2.   Peter Randall, *Bullying in Adulthood: Assessing the Bullies and Their Victims* (New York: Taylor & Francis, 2001); Gary and Ruth Namie, *The Bully at Work: What You Can Do to Stop the Hurt and Reclaim Your Dignity on the Job,* 2nd ed. (Naperville, IL: Sourcebooks, 2009).

INDEX

Note: Page numbers ending in "f" refer to figures. Page numbers ending in "t" refer to tables.